DUPLICATE PAIRS FOR YOU

by ANDREW KAMBITES
in the *Master Bridge Series*

Understanding Acol: the Good Bidding Guide (with Eric Crowhurst)

Task-Masters

Strategic Acol Bidding
Overcalling in Acol (with Pat Husband)
Improve Your Acol Bidding (with Pat Husband)
Strong Twos, Pre-Empts and Slams (with Pat Husband)

DUPLICATE PAIRS FOR YOU

Andrew Kambites

London
VICTOR GOLLANCZ LTD
in association with
PETER CRAWLEY
1991

First published in Great Britain 1991
in association with Peter Crawley
by Victor Gollancz Ltd
14 Henrietta Street, London WC2E 8QJ

A catalogue record for this book
is available from the British Library

ISBN 0 575 05108 6

Photoset in Great Britain by
Rowland Phototypesetting Ltd, Bury St Edmunds, Suffolk
and printed by St Edmundsbury Press Ltd
Bury St Edmunds, Suffolk

Contents

Introduction   7

1. Scoring at Pairs   9

PART 1   GENERAL BIDDING TACTICS

2. The Right Denomination in an
   Uncontested Auction   13
3. Part-Score Auctions   19
4. More Bidding Decisions   27

PART 2   BIDDING CONVENTIONS

5. Your Choice of System   38
6. The Crowhurst Convention   43
7. Transfer Bidding   48
8. Takeout Doubles   56
9. Two-Suited Overcalls   67
10. Opponents Interfere over Partner's 1NT   75
11. The Multi-Coloured 2♦ Bid   80

PART 3   DECLARER PLAY

12. Declarer Play When the Hand is
    Progressing Normally   87
13. Declarer Play if Progress Differs from
    Other Tables   91
14. Gracefully Accepting Defeat   98

PART 4   DEFENSIVE PLAY

15. Defensive Counting   103
16. General Defensive Duplicate Tactics   112
17. Signals and Discards   123
18. Modern Lead Systems   132

19. Creating Tops and Bottoms   140

Introduction

To thousands of bridge players the duplicate pairs form of the game is addictive. Players who have enjoyed rubber bridge in their own homes for years can suddenly become hooked on the combination of skill and luck that is unique to duplicate pairs. The fact that the strong pair consistently does well even if it is dealt inferior cards, while occasionally its weaker brethren enjoy a moment of triumph, is a fascinating part of the duplicate scene. Even those whose main purpose is to participate in the competitive friendship of a duplicate club soon yearn to improve their own game, and this book is devoted to such 'improvers'. I firmly believe that almost all bridge enthusiasts can find enjoyment in duplicate pairs, thus the title *Duplicate Pairs for You*.

Generally speaking it is not possible to become a strong duplicate player until you have mastered general bridge principles. Indeed, if you try to graft the material of this book onto unsure foundations do not imagine that you will become a winner! Assuming you have acquired a sound grasp of the basics of bidding and card play, if you then want to be a 'good' duplicate player you need to adjust your style and tactics to the somewhat artificial match-pointing method which I describe in chapter 1. In particular, you must be adaptable and prepared to take risks. If you are over-squeamish about venturing featherweight overcalls, making borderline penalty doubles, or risking the defeat of your contract in the pursuit of a meagre overtrick, you will not fulfil your potential.

Except in chapter 19 where you will see how to tackle a hand with the intention of creating an abnormal result, I assume that you start each hand aiming to play percentage duplicate bridge. As the bidding and early card play develop you will often have good reason to believe that you are heading for a poor score, perhaps through no fault of your own. In that case it can be necessary to take desperate measures to pull something out of the ruins. Alternatively, you might be aware that the hand is developing in a manner which is favourable to you. Perhaps you are in a particularly good contract that other pairs will not have reached, or you have been given a cheap trick by the defenders, or your opponents have clearly allowed you to get away with murder in the auction. Then you will not take any unnecessary risks to jeopardise your good fortune, and, indeed, a safety play to ensure your contract may be appropriate. To react in this way to the ebb and flow of events on a particular hand *is* percentage duplicate bridge, even though some of the hair-raising tactics I recommend would justifiably give the rubber bridge specialist a nervous breakdown!

The main part of *Duplicate Pairs for You* is divided into four sections.

i) Chapters 2–4 introduce you to the special tactical bidding considerations of the pairs game.

ii) Chapters 5–11 describe conventional bidding themes that are currently fashionable. Not only do you need to understand them in order to counter their use by your opponents, but if you adopt them, having systematically discussed them with your partner, your own game will improve dramatically.

iii) Chapters 12–14 describe why it may not be good enough to simply fulfil your contract as declarer.

iv) Chapters 15–18 deal with defensive card play. The theme of defensive counting is investigated in chapter 15, because you cannot achieve much without it! Then, after general defensive tactics have been examined in chapter 16, you are introduced to modern systems of leading, signalling, and discarding.

1. Scoring at Pairs

Filling in the travelling score sheet

The most noticeable difference between duplicate pairs and rubber bridge is that each hand is complete in itself. Whatever you achieve, a score is worked out for the hand, and the next hand is scored completely independently. Therefore you always need to bid a contract that would score 100 below the line at rubber bridge to score a game bonus. You cannot accumulate part-scores towards a game. In fact this makes bidding far simpler, as almost all bidding systems are designed with no part-scores in mind. The concept of not passing 13-point hands is based upon the idea that if both players passed with such values a game hand might be lost. Passing out a part-score is unfortunate, but passing out a game is not acceptable. A bidding system designed to cope with 60 below the line would probably recommend that you always open with 11 points!

The vulnerability of each hand is predetermined by markings on the board. In any set of four boards, one will be played at *Love all*, one at *Game all*, one with only North/South vulnerable, and one with only East/West vulnerable. Scoring is similar to rubber bridge, but 'above the line' and 'below the line' scores are gathered together. Additionally:

i) Bidding and making a non-vulnerable game scores a bonus of 300. If the game is vulnerable the bonus is 500. Thus 4♡ + 1 (meaning 4♡ making with an overtrick) scores 450 if not vulnerable, and 650 if vulnerable.

ii) Bidding and making a part-score scores a bonus of 50, irrespective of the vulnerability. Thus 2♡ + 2 (meaning 2♡ making with two overtricks) scores 170.

iii) If you fail to make a doubled, non-vulnerable contract by four tricks or more the penalties are increased. Four off costs 800 (not 700), five off costs 1100 (not 900) and each additional doubled undertrick costs an extra 300.

iv) A successful redoubled contract scores 100 'for the insult', not 50.

v) 'Honours' are not scored. Quite reasonably, it is decided that if you are lucky enough to possess four or five top trumps, or all four aces in a no-trump contract, it is rubbing salt into your opponents' wounds to reward you further!

Match-pointing

The scoring described above is only the first step in calculating the winning pair. At the end of an evening's duplicate each board will have its travelling score sheet looking like the table below, except that the last two columns will still be blank.

Board 8									
NS	EW	Contract	By	Tricks	N/S score		Match points		
					+	−	NS		EW
1	5	4S doubled	S	10	590		10		0
2	7	4S − 1	S	9		50	1		9
3									
4									
5									
6	8	3NT − 1	N	8		50	1		9
7									
8									
9	10	3NT + 1	N	10	430		7		3
10									
11	3	2C + 2	N	10	130		4		6
12	4	3NT + 1	N	10	430		7		3

Completing the traveller then becomes the responsibility of the person who is running the event, the *director*. He fills in the last two columns, giving each pair two *Match-Points* for every pair playing the same cards that they have beaten, and one match-point for every pair with whom they have tied. Here, pair 1 get 10 match-points because their score is better than the scores achieved by pairs 2, 6, 9, 11 and 12. Pairs 9 and 12 each get 7 match-points because they outscored 2, 6 and 11 and they tied with each other. Pair 11 get 4 match-points for outscoring pairs 2 and 6. Pairs 2 and 6 get only 1 match-point, for tying with each other.

Pair 1 is said to have an outright *Top* score because they scored the maximum possible number of match-points on the board. Pairs 2 and 6 have a shared *Bottom*. To calculate any East/West score just subtract the match-point score of their North/South opponents from the outright top (in this case 10.)

Match-Points are the hard currency of duplicate pairs, and you will realise that you don't automatically score any match-points for just bidding to the correct contract and making it. If you score +600 for bidding and making a vulnerable 3NT you would feel content at rubber bridge, but if every other pair scores +630 by making an overtrick in the same contract you will score a complete *Bottom*, (zero match-points) and your opponents will get a *Top*.

Playing rubber bridge the main decision is whether your combined assets justify part-score, game or slam. Once that decision is made any successful contract is acceptable, the difference between a vulnerable 3NT + 1 (630) and 5 ◇ (600) being negligible. Similarly, failing to find your sacrifice in 3 ♠ − 1 (−100) over your opponents' 3 ♡ (−140) is of little consequence. At duplicate pairs these minor differences of score can assume exaggerated importance, and your tactics must be altered significantly to allow for this. Inevitably, the somewhat artificial match-pointing method requires a certain amount of adjustment, both in bidding and card play, and investigating that is the main purpose of this book.

Mej >

My No NH

CK SCORE
CHART

Sometims MIRER INO
IS
BEST

Part 1   General Bidding Tactics

2. The Right Denomination in an Uncontested Auction

Major suit or no trumps?

The pecking order between a major suit contract and no trumps is well illustrated by the hand below in which only East/West are vulnerable. Assume the contract is played at game level, although the same arguments would apply in a part-score or slam.

a) West   East
    ♠ 8 5   ♠ A Q J 7
    ♡ A Q J 10 7   ♡ 9 8 4 3
    ♢ 8 5 4   ♢ A K
    ♣ A K 2   ♣ 8 5 4

Declarer (West) has finesses to take in both major suits.

If both are successful (25% of the time) twelve tricks are available in no trumps (3 spades, 5 hearts, 2 diamonds and 2 clubs) for a score of +690. Alternatively, all thirteen tricks can be made if hearts are trumps for +710. (The extra trick comes from ruffing the ♢ 8 in dummy.)

If one is successful (50% of the time) you will make 3NT + 2 (+660) or 4♡ + 2 (+680).

If both fail you will make at most ten tricks in 3NT (+630), perhaps even failing if you risk both finesses and opponents end up cashing diamond winners, but eleven tricks are still easy in hearts (+650).

Plainly the heart contract is far superior, giving lie to the commonly-held fallacy that it is always right to play in no trumps. Indeed, it is even more important to seek out the eight-card major fit in duplicate pairs than in rubber bridge because there is so often one extra trick available (perhaps through ruffing a loser in the hand with short trumps, perhaps because the trump suit allows you to control the play sufficiently to set up your long suit before the defenders manage to establish their winners.)

Minor suit or no trumps?

Now reconsider the previous hand with the red suits exchanged.

b) West   East
    ♠ 8 5   ♠ A Q J 7
    ♡ 8 5 4   ♡ A K
    ◇ A Q J 10 7   ◇ 9 8 4 3
    ♣ A K 2   ♣ 8 5 4

The same type of analysis this time leads to a very different conclusion!

With both finesses working, +640 for 5◇ + 2 compares very unfavourably with +690 for 3NT + 3. Equally, if just one finesse works +620 for 5◇ + 1 cannot compete in the matchpoint stakes with +660 for 3NT + 2. Only for the meagre 25% of the time when both finesses fail is +600 for 5◇ made likely to equal, or outscore 3NT, when a heart lead may defeat declarer if he greedily takes the spade finesse in the quest for overtricks. Of course the best contract is 6◇, which succeeds 75% of the time!

To summarise, it is correct to seek a major suit fit rather than automatically play in no trumps, but minor suit contracts should be preferred only if you have no reasonable alternative. This is particularly true at game level, (though if you can successfully uncover a good minor suit slam with only 30 HCP you are certain to score well.) For this reason, when you have a good minor suit it is frequently best to abandon an over-scientific approach to bidding and choose the direct route to 3NT, giving your opponents as few clues as possible! For example, partner opens a weak 1NT and you have:

♠ 5 3   ♡ 8 4 2   ◇ A   ♣ A K Q 8 6 4 3

5♣, or even 6♣, may be better than 3NT, but 3NT is the winning duplicate bid. A favourable lead may give you the first twelve tricks when the defenders could have collected the first five! There is no point in scientifically discovering a spade weakness and settling in a laydown 5♣ (scoring only 600, having pinpointed the successful spade lead to the defenders) and then

bitterly bemoaning your misfortune as the rest of the field hacks
its way to 3NT, making 690 when the opening leader fails to
diagnose that a spade lead from ♠ A 6 2 could defeat the
contract. That is part of the game!

However, it can be important sometimes to be able to investigate a minor suit *slam* and still be able to settle in 4NT if
unsuccessful.

c)	West	East		West	East
	♠ A K Q	♠ 4		1◇	1♡
	♡ Q 3 2	♡ A K 5 4		3NT	4◇
	◇ Q J 8 2	◇ A 9 5 4		4NT	
	♣ K Q 3	♣ 9 8 7 2			

East correctly introduces his major suit rather than give immediate support to diamonds, but is faced with a typical pairs dilemma
after West's strong rebid. 6◇ may be an excellent contract with
only 30 HCP, provided West holds good red cards and not too
many wasted values in spades. East is confident that if his slam
try is unsuccessful then 4NT will be a safe haven, so he removes
3NT into 4◇. This is unconditionally forcing, as taking 3NT out
into 4♣ or 4◇ is always forcing unless 3NT has been doubled.
But with so many of his values in the black suits West is not
inclined to be co-operative and bids a *natural* 4NT. It is a good
pairs tactic to agree with partner that if a minor suit has been bid
and supported, then 4NT over 4♣ or 4◇ is to *play*, NOT
Blackwood, unless one partner has made a cue bid. In hand c)
West would have continued with 4♠ if interested in a diamond
slam, enabling East to continue with a Blackwood 4NT if he
considered it appropriate.

While a minor suit slam with relatively few points will score
well, if you bid an 'obvious' slam you should consider 6NT as an
alternative to your agreed suit. With the hand below you are
delighted, and somewhat amazed, to hear your partner open
1◇. You naturally launch into Blackwood 4NT, and are rather
disappointed to hear the 5♡ response, showing that an ace is
missing. Before sadly settling for 6◇, try asking for kings with
5NT. If he shows a king (the ♡ K) 6NT must be laydown.

Partner should not assume you are guaranteeing that all the aces are present and bid a grand slam!

♠ K Q   ♡ Q   ◇ K Q 7 6 5 3 2   ♣ A K 3

Note that the above example would be just as valid if the 'agreed' suit was a major. If you can tell that exactly 12 tricks are available in hearts or no trumps, pick the higher scoring denomination! It is even possible in similar situations that the no-trump contract may be the only making slam! Suppose you bid a slam with 35 HCP, but with an ace missing and ♡ K Q 3 2 opposite ♡ A 6 5 4. Played in hearts you are without resource if trumps break 4-1, but played in no trumps you may have 12 easy tricks!

Principles of choosing the denomination at pairs

In the early part of the auction the desirability of finding a major suit fit only reinforces principles that apply also in rubber bridge. It is certainly *not* correct to distort your bidding by attempting to find a major fit, for example with a) open 1◇ (your longest suit) and if necessary rebid 2◇, relying on partner to introduce hearts if he has four. Equally with b) open 1♠ and rebid 2◇ over 2♣. It is pointless to rebid 2♠ just because it is pairs, especially as your 2◇ rebid promises a five-card spade suit!

a) ♠ K 6   ♡ A J 8 4   ◇ A J 8 4 2   ♣ J 7
b) ♠ A Q 8 4 3   ♡ K 6   ◇ K J 6 2   ♣ 8 3

The following points are worth a mention.

i) If you stick with the modern Acol principles of opening the *lower* of touching four-card suits with a 4-4-3-2-shape hand too strong to open 1NT (intending a no-trump rebid unless the response is in your other suit), you won't miss a major suit fit and hence won't go far wrong. However, there are conflicting opinions about what to open if the suits are *not* touching. If you open 1♣ with c) you can rebid 1♡ over 1◇, or 2NT over 1♠. Alternatively, if you open 1♡ you can rebid 2NT over 1♠ or 3NT over 2◇. Playing rubber bridge it doesn't matter much, but playing duplicate it is marginally better to get in your major suit before your *opponents* bid 1♠! In chapter 6 you will meet exceptions!

c)   ♠ K 2   ♡ K 7 4 2   ◇ K J 8   ♣ A K 7 3

ii) You should never conceal a four-card major suit which can be bid at the one level. The correct response to 1◇ is 1♠ with hands d), e) or f). The point with f) is that you are not strong enough to continue if partner rebids 2◇, so as you are worth only one bid show your major suit.

d)   ♠ J 8 5 3   ♡ A 6 2   ◇ 8 6 3   ♣ K 8 5
e)   ♠ J 8 5 3   ♡ A 6   ◇ K 8 6 3   ♣ 9 8 3
f)   ♠ J 8 5 3   ♡ 7 5   ◇ K 8   ♣ K J 7 5 3

iii) If you have a four-card major and enough to invite game opposite a 1NT opening bid, use Stayman rather than just hack 3NT.

iv) You should prefer to raise partner's major suit to the two-level with three-card support and a doubleton, rather than respond 1NT. Raise 1♠ to 2♠ with hand g). Not only is 2♠ likely to score better than 1NT with the aid of a club ruff in dummy (even if partner has only four spades), but support may help partner to compete successfully to 3♠ if opponents bid at the three-level.

g)   ♠ J 8 6   ♡ A 6 5 3   ◇ 8 6 3 2   ♣ K 8

v) If you are weak it is best to prefer a 1NT response to a dubious 2♣ or 2◇ change of suit. Respond 1NT to partner's 1♠ with hand h). In theory you are one point too strong for a 6-9 HCP 1NT response, but your hand seems to fit badly with partner and the necessary 2NT continuation over a 2♣ or 2♡ response may prove too high for comfort. Because of the danger of responder having a singleton, or even void, in his suit, opener must *never* sign off in a five-card suit after a 1NT response to 1◇, 1♡ or 1♠.

Sometimes it is even tactically desirable to *rebid* 1NT with a singleton in partner's suit rather than introduce a minor suit at the two level! With i) open 1◇, and over the predictable 1♠ response rebid 1NT at pairs.

h)   ♠ 9   ♡ K J 6   ◇ Q 9 7 5 3   ♣ K J 7 4
i)   ♠ J   ♡ A Q 6   ◇ K J 7 3 2   ♣ A J 6 2

vi) False preference to a major becomes even more attractive than usual. You correctly respond 1NT to partner's 1♠ with hand j), and his rebid is 2◇. His sequence shows at least 5 spades so give preference to 2♠.

j)　　♠ K 8　　　♡ A 10 8　　　◇ J 7 4 3　　　♣ 10 9 7 5

Quiz

1) You are playing simple Acol, with a weak no trump, Blackwood, and Stayman. For each of these hands at *Love all* state how you would respond to an opening bid of:

　　i) 1◇　　　ii) 1♠　　　iii) 1NT

a)	♠ K 5 3 2	♡ A J 7	◇ 9 8 5	♣ A 8 4
b)	♠ J 8 6	♡ K 4 3 2	◇ K 6	♣ 7 4 3 2
c)	♠ Q J 7 2	♡ 8 6	◇ 9 8	♣ A J 10 6 2
d)	♠ Q J 7 2	♡ A 6	◇ J 8	♣ A J 10 6 2
e)	♠ Q 7	♡ K 2	◇ 9 5	♣ A K Q 9 7 5 2
f)	♠ K 7 3	♡ 4 3 2	◇ 9	♣ A J 5 4 3 2

Answers to quiz

a) i) 1♠. Show your four-card major. Bid 2NT next time.

ii) 3♠. Obvious.

iii) 2♣. Look for the 4-4 major suit fit before committing yourself to no trumps.

b) i) 1♡. Show your major suit.

ii) 2♠. Better than 1NT with three spades and a side suit doubleton.

iii) Pass. You cannot use Stayman as a 2◇ reply will leave you with nowhere to go.

c) i) 1♠. You are not strong enough for two bids so show your major suit.

ii) 3♠. The value bid.

iii) Pass. Again you are too weak for Stayman.

d) i) 2♣. This time you are strong enough for two bids so start with your longer suit and bid spades next time.

ii) 2♣. Start a delayed game raise.

iii) 2♣. Look for the major suit fit. You will see in chapter 7 that if you play transfer bids you can investigate a fit in either black suit, but for the time being the major takes priority.

e) i) and ii) 2♣. 3NT looks attractive, but it would be premature. If opener has a better than minimum opening bid, a slam is worth investigating.

iii) 3NT. Don't tell your opponents what to lead!

f) i) 1NT. A more practical response than 2♣, after which you would have to pass a 2◇ rebid.

ii) 2♣, intending to support spades next time. You are too strong for 2♠, and an immediate 3♠ shows four-card support.

iii) 2♣. Intending to sign off in 3♣ next time. Don't carry the no-trump infatuation too far!

3. Part-Score Auctions

Competing aggressively

In duplicate pairs part-score contracts command a far greater importance than in rubber bridge, because there are the same number of match-points at stake on every hand, whether each side has a boring, balanced, combined 20 HCP, or whether a vulnerable grand slam is at stake. The important point to grasp is that the majority of part-score results lie between 100 and 200. (eg. 2♠, 1♠ + 1 or 2♣ + 1 each score 110, 1NT + 1 scores 120, and at the other end of the range even 3♠ + 1 scores only 170 or 2NT + 2 only 180.) Therefore, if the balance of strength lies with your side on a part-score deal, a score of +200 is likely to be excellent, whereas a score of only +100 will probably be inadequate. At rubber bridge it would be madness to take risks to turn −140 into −100, but such tactics are an acknowledged part of the expert duplicate game. In particular, allowing your non-vulnerable opponents to drift two off undoubled in 1NT or 2♡ (+100) when you could have made 3♠ (+140) is almost guaranteed to give you a poor score. This sort of reasoning makes it essential that you compete aggressively in the battle for the part-scores, taking reasonable risks to snatch the contract yourself or push opponents from a safe resting spot to a precarious one.

Light opening bids and overcalls

Light opening bids and overcalls are desirable, provided you have a suit that you want partner to lead if your side loses the auction. If your suit has poor quality you should pass with a hand of borderline opening strength, because even if you succeed in pushing your opponents one level higher you might persuade partner to give back the trick on the opening lead. At teams the higher level would cancel out such a lead, but at pairs conceding 140 rather that 110 can be a disaster. If in doubt, ask whether you want partner to lead your suit from a holding like K x.

At love all open 1♠ with a) or b), and be prepared to overcall your right hand opponent's 1♣ with 1♠ if you hold c). The great merit of a 1♠ overcall with c) is that it may make it hard for the enemy to find a 4-4 heart fit. A 1♠ overcall of 1♡ would be less attractive, indeed light overcalls are always more effective if they have the pre-emptive effect of bypassing a major suit. Even having only a four-card suit should not deter you if other conditions are favourable. Overcall 1♣ with 1♠ if you hold d).

a)	♠ A K 8 5 3	♡ 9	◇ Q J 9 6	♣ 8 5 3
b)	♠ A Q J 8 5 2	♡ 9	◇ Q 10 9 8	♣ 5 3
c)	♠ A Q 10 9 8	♡ 9 5	◇ 10 9 8	♣ 9 5 2
d)	♠ A Q J 7	♡ 9 7 4	◇ 9 5 2	♣ A 7 3

When you are vulnerable a little more caution is necessary. If you are not vulnerable one down doubled or two down undoubled (−100) can be a triumph if opponents can make 140. But the same results cost −200 if you are vulnerable, a score justifiably known as the 'kiss of death'! Your opponents, knowing this, will be more inclined to chance a speculative double.

Note that light opening bids are especially attractive in third seat, but be wary of opening light in fourth position, particularly if you hold the minor suits. You are too likely to start a competitive auction which you will lose to an enemy major fit. A good rule of thumb is to only open in fourth seat if your total of HCP and spades comes to at least 15.

Thus pass with e) in fourth seat, and if you must open with f),
3♦ is best.

e) ♠ 8   ♡ K 7 5   ♦ K J 5 4 3   ♣ K Q 8 5
f) ♠ 8   ♡ K 7   ♦ K Q J 9 8 6   ♣ Q J 10 8

Protection, and speculative doubles

It is rarely correct to allow opponents to snatch the contract at a
low level if they have found a fit. The following auction is typical
of a high-quality pairs game at *Love all*.

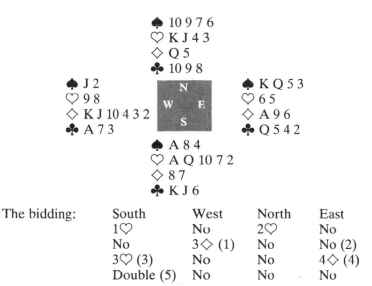

```
                    ♠ 10 9 7 6
                    ♡ K J 4 3
                    ♦ Q 5
                    ♣ 10 9 8
   ♠ J 2                          ♠ K Q 5 3
   ♡ 9 8           N              ♡ 6 5
   ♦ K J 10 4 3 2  W   E          ♦ A 9 6
   ♣ A 7 3           S            ♣ Q 5 4 2
                    ♠ A 8 4
                    ♡ A Q 10 7 2
                    ♦ 8 7
                    ♣ K J 6
```

The bidding:

	South	West	North	East
	1♡	No	2♡	No
	No	3♦ (1)	No	No (2)
	3♡ (3)	No	No	4♦ (4)
	Double (5)	No	No	No

1) West knows East has some good cards. At love all he certainly
doesn't intend to sell out to 2♡, indeed he might be tempted to
protect with this hand even if vulnerable!
2) East knows West is protecting and doesn't let a few good
cards go to his head.
3) These types of auction tend to die at the three level, and are
therefore often won by the side with the higher-ranking suit.
South doesn't know whether either 3♦, or 3♡, or both contracts
are making, but 3♡ is only wrong in the unlikely event that
neither contract makes.

4) A slightly risky venture, hoping to escape for −100 or less: Note that −100 may score reasonably well even if 3♡ fails because some North/South pairs may have been allowed to play peacefully in 2♡, scoring 110.

5) This would be very risky at rubber bridge as South cannot be sure of beating 4◇. However, he feels that he has had his pocket picked, and rightly believes that 4◇ making will give him a very poor score, whether it is doubled or not! Therefore he tries to salvage something from the wreckage.

Note that if North finds the club lead his side should beat 4◇ doubled by two tricks, for 300 and an excellent score. Otherwise East/West will be reasonably content with −100, beating East/West pairs conceding −110 against 2♡. It is frequently correct to try a close penalty double if you feel your plus score has been stolen by an enemy bid that other pairs won't find, particularly if opponents are vulnerable, giving the possibility of the magic +200!

The theme of doubling rather than accepting a small plus score can also be seen if an opponent's overcall deprives you of your bid. As North at *Game all* you hold:

♠ 9 4   ♡ K 10 4   ◇ A J 6 3   ♣ Q 6 5 2

i)	South	West	North	ii)	South	West	North
	1NT	2♡	?		1♠	2♡	?

In either case a penalty double would be a reasonable gamble at duplicate pairs. Firstly, although you hold the balance of strength you have no suitable alternative, and even +100 may score poorly if you can make +110 from 2♠ or +120 from 1NT + 1. Secondly, if you can achieve +200, that might be an outright top. Thirdly, if you do double West into game you have probably done no more than turn a poor score into a bottom. Therefore although you cannot be totally confident of beating 2♡ doubled, the potential gain outweighs the loss. It is true to say that if you never double your opponents into game at pairs you must be letting them get away with murder!

Note again that a risky double is always more attractive if they are vulnerable, because the rewards for one off are so much greater. Turning 100 into 200 in a part-score auction when your side has the balance of strength is likely to have a dramatic effect on your score, but turning 50 into 100 may make very little difference. It is the *second* non-vulnerable doubled undertrick that makes the difference. If they are vulnerable you should double if you think that you have a significantly greater chance of defeating them than they have of making the contract, but if they are not vulnerable a good rule of thumb for doubling is that you should believe that you have as good a chance of two off as they have of making it.

By now you should be getting the two-edged message; bid aggressively in the protective position and don't hesitate to double if opponents take liberties. However, there are situations when you must be very wary of protecting:

Supposing South's opening 1♣ at love all is passed round to you with these hands:

a)   ♠ 6   ♡ K 8 3   ◇ K Q J 5 3 2   ♣ 7 4 3
b)   ♠ 6   ♡ K 8 6 3   ◇ Q 8 6 2   ♣ A Q J 2
c)   ♠ A Q 5   ♡ K 6 4 2   ◇ Q 8 6   ♣ J 8 3
d)   ♠ K 7 5 4 2   ♡ 9 7   ◇ A J 7   ♣ 9 7 3
e)   ♠ K 7 5 2   ♡ 9 7 5 3   ◇ A J 7 3   ♣ 2

It is very dangerous to bid 1◇ with a), as it is quite likely that North/South will discover a superior spade fit, or even settle in a higher scoring no-trump contract. If partner had reasonable spades and opening values he would surely have competed, therefore either he is very weak, or your opponents have the spade suit. If you must protect with a) try 3◇ which at least gives you a sporting chance of closing the auction. With b) any protective noise is dubious because far too many of your high cards are concentrated in their suit. A 12–16 point 1NT with c) (it doesn't promise a club guard), 1♠ with d), and a takeout double with e) are worthwhile.

The other time when protection is dangerous is when opponents have made several bids but *haven't* found a fit.

South	West	North	East
1♡	No	1♠	No
2◇	No	2♠	No
No	?		

West should be very cautious now! North/South may be in a poor

6-1 fit, but have as many as 24 HCP. It is always safer to protect against a known fit, firstly because the probability of your side having a fit is greater, and secondly because there is less danger that opponents are underbidding because of a misfit.

Of course protection is equally important for the opening side. As South at love all you open 1 ♠ and face this dilemma when the bidding returns to you.

♠ K Q 7 5 3	South	West	North	East
♡ K J 6	1♠	2♣	No	No
♢ A Q 10 2	?			
♣ 4				

It cannot be right to sell out to 2♣, and a takeout double is preferable to 2♢ because it might enable partner to bring his heart suit into play. This is just the sort of hand that will play well in a 4-3 heart fit because clubs can be trumped in the hand with *short* trumps, thereby keeping control. Yet again at pairs, being prepared to play in a 4-3 major suit fit may be the key to a good score.

Note that a re-opening double by South is for takeout, not penalties. The criteria that distinguish takeout doubles from penalty doubles are explained on p. 56, but they are based on common sense. Exchange South's club and diamond holdings and he would have no good reason to make a penalty double of a low level club contract. Firstly, he might succeed in driving East/ West into a better denomination, and secondly, 2♣ may be laydown if North has nothing. As you will see later, in the world of duplicate pairs experts tend to allocate an increasing number of doubles for takeout; not only those that are traditional Acol takeout doubles (like these), but also a new breed of conventional competitive doubles that are examined in chapter 8.

An aggressive re-opening double with the hand above would be equally correct after either of these sequences:

South	West	North	East		South	West	North	East
1♠	2♣	No	3♣					1♣
?					1♠	3♣	No	No
					?			

In each case double is for takeout because both of these conditions are satisfied:

   i) A *suit* bid has been doubled at, or below, the three level.

   ii) Partner has done no more than pass.

Your choice of competitive bid

When you have a choice of reasonable bids, pick the bid that will make it easiest for partner to get into the auction. Consider these hands if your right-hand opponent opens 1♡ at *Love all.*

a)	♠ K 6 2	♡ 8 4	♢ A Q 6	♣ A J 8 3 2
b)	♠ A J 8 3 2	♡ 8	♢ A Q 6	♣ K 6 3 2
c)	♠ A J 6 2	♡ 8 6 2	♢ A Q 6	♣ Q 6 2

With a) or b) you can either double, or bid your suit. If you double it is more likely that partner can compete with 6 HCP if your left-hand opponent raises to 2♡. That sways the balance of argument in favour of a double with a), but b) is slightly more difficult. The other side of the coin is that if you overcall *you* can make a takeout double next time, but if you double you cannot bid spades protectively without showing a stronger hand than this. The unpalatable fact is that if you choose to double you will *never* find a 5-3 spade fit. There are several reasons why this is far more damaging than losing a minor suit. Not only does the major fit score better, but if both sides find a fit you can outbid them at the three level if your suit is higher ranking, whereas with clubs you would have to proceed to four level with the greater risk of being doubled.

   Your desire to push your way into the auction is so great that it would not be unreasonable to make a takeout double of 1♡ with c), an action that would be insane at rubber bridge. However I don't recommend it if you are vulnerable.

Quiz

1) What is your call with these hands:

   i) As third hand after two passes at *Green* vulnerability (i.e., only your opponents are vulnerable).

   ii) At *Green* vulnerability after your right-hand opponent has opened 1♢ as dealer?

iii) At *Red* vulnerability (i.e. only your side is vulnerable) after your right-hand opponent has opened 1♡ as dealer?

a) ♠ A Q 7 6 3   ♡ 9 4 2   ◇ K 3   ♣ 9 8 4
b) ♠ J 7 5 4 2   ♡ J 8   ◇ A K Q   ♣ 9 7 4
c) ♠ K Q 4   ♡ Q J 9   ◇ J 4   ♣ A 8 7 4 2

2) What do you bid with the hand below after each of these auctions:

♠ 9   ♡ Q J 8 5 2   ◇ K 6 4   ♣ K 8 5 2?

	Love all					*Love all*		
a)	South	West	North	East	b)	South	West	North	East
	1♠	No	No	?		1♣	No	No	?

	East/West Game					*East/West Game*		
c)	South	West	North	East	d)	South	West	North	East
	1♠	No	1NT	No		1◇	No	2◇	No
	2♣	No	2◇	No		No	?		
	No	?							

3) What do you bid with the hand below after each of these auctions:

♠ K Q 10   ♡ 7 2   ◇ K 10 9 6   ♣ 9 7 5 2

	Game all					*Game all*		
a)	South	West	North	East	b)	South	West	North	East
	1NT	2◇	?			1♡	2◇	?	

	Game all					*North/South Game*		
c)	South	West	North	East	d)	South	West	North	East
	1♠	No	2♠	No		1◇	3♡	4◇	4♡
	No	3♡	No	No		5◇	No	No	5♡
	3♠	No	No	4♡		No	No	?	
	No	No	?						

Answers to quiz

1) a) i) 1♠. Pre-emptive and lead-directing.
   ii) 1♠. Cutting out the heart suit.

      iii) Pass. This time the vulnerability is wrong and 1♠ has no pre-emptive value over 1♡.

  b) i), ii) and iii). All pass. Attracting a spade lead against an enemy contract could give away a vital overtrick.

  c) i) 1NT. Pre-emptive as well as constructive.
      ii) Double. Cheeky, but it pays to push aggressively into the auction at green vulnerability.
      iii) Pass. You must be joking!

2) a) Double. Slightly more flexible than 2♡.
  b) Pass. Ask yourself 'Who has the spades?'
  c) Pass. Too dangerous! They seem to have a misfit.
  d) 2♡. Partner has some HCP and this time they have found a good fit, so give them a little push.

3) a), b), c), and d) all double. Don't be satisfied with +100 or less. If these contracts make you are unlikely to get a good score anyway!

4. More Bidding Decisions

Deciding the level

General speaking it is unsound tactics to push too hard at pairs for thin slams. The slam may be 50%, making it borderline in theory, but in practice there is usually at least one pair in a stupid contract, e.g., a part-score, or the wrong game contract, so it is as well to achieve a sensible plus score to ensure beating them.

    Grand slams should be avoided like the plague unless you are *very* sure, because bidding the small slam is likely to be sufficient to ensure a respectable score. It is by no means unknown for a pair to suffer the frustration of failing in an excellent grand slam because of a 4-1 trump break, only to find the rest of the field in game!

By the same logic you will probably gain more than you lose over a long period of time by avoiding borderline game contracts, unlike rubber bridge or teams of four for which the scoring system makes it highly desirable to attempt a game contract which depends only on a finesse.

Another point that might not have occurred to you is that you should be more inclined to take the last plunge to game, than to initiate a game try. Compare these auctions:

i) West   East   ii) West   East
    1♠   3♠   1♠   2♠
    ?   ?

If you raise to 4♠ with a borderline hand after auction i) there is one good outcome (making it) and one bad (failing). On the other hand, if you make a game try after ii) there is the same plus, but this time two minuses. Partner might raise to 4♠ and fail, or he might fail in 3♠!

Note that even if you consider your card play sufficiently superior to believe you will make an extra trick, that will suffice to give you a top even if you are in the part-score.

Good and bad points

When playing duplicate pairs there is great scope for recognising 'good' and 'bad' points and backing your judgement. In particular, any pair that understand the following principles will do well.

i) If your high cards are in your *long* suits the hand is more suitable for playing than defending, and you should bid positively in the uncontested auction. Paradoxically, the opposite is true if your high cards are concentrated in your *short* suits. Then the hand is more suitable for defending, and you should err on the side of caution in the uncontested auction. The principles already given in chapter 3 for light opening bids and overcalls are just one example of this. You probably already make some adjustments to your bidding: not giving singleton honours their full point value, and deducting points for holdings like doubleton K Q, or Q J. Nevertheless, you should try to develop your senses to a higher level than this.

As an example, compare the value of these hands after the auction following:

South	West	North	East
1♡	2♣	4♡	5♣
?			

a) ♠ A 9 7 4   ♡ A K 8 5 4 3   ◇ 6 2   ♣ 4
b) ♠ 9 7 4 2   ♡ 9 8 7 5 4 3   ◇ A K   ♣ A

With a) bid 5♡. You have excellent *playing* strength, because your high cards are promoting to winning rank minor honours your partner might have in the major suits. On the other hand your *defensive* strength is very limited, as one opponent might ruff the ♡ A! It is by no means impossible that 5♣ and 5♡ both make! Conversely, with b) you should double. Your high cards are promoting nothing and you are virtually guaranteed three defensive tricks.

ii) Isolated honour cards, particularly queens and jacks, are seldom worth their point count. Which of the two hands below makes the better 1NT opening at Game All?

c) ♠ 9 4 3   ♡ 8 4 2   ◇ A K 6 3   ♣ K Q 4
d) ♠ K 4 3   ♡ A 8 2   ◇ Q 6 4 3   ♣ K 7 4

If you think d) is better because it has guards in each suit you would not be alone in being wrong! The number one aim of declaring a contract is to *make tricks* and c) has more trick-taking potential than d). In c) your high cards reinforce each other, and in particular your diamond honours will be helpful in the quest to establish a length trick in this suit. To understand the concept of 'reinforcement' compare the suit holdings below:

West	East
♠ K Q 2	♠ 5 4 3
♡ K 5 2	♡ Q 4 3
◇ K 5 2	◇ 6 4 3
♣ Q 5 2	♣ 6 4 3

In the major suits you hold exactly the same high cards, but you will make two spade tricks if South has the ♠ A, whereas you are most unlikely to score two heart tricks unless your opponents help you. Your combined minor suit holdings are the equal of either major suit, but you cannot be sure of making even one minor suit trick! The difference is that the ♠ K and ♠ Q *reinforce* each other by being in the same suit, and in the same hand. The ◇ K and ♣ Q do nothing to reinforce each other.

Now consider your continuation with hand e) if partner opens 1♡ and rebids 2♡ over your 2◇ response:

e) ♠ Q 8 4   ♡ A 7 4   ◇ Q 9 7 5 2   ♣ Q 6

It would not be at all unreasonable at pairs to devalue your unattractive queen-high suits and pass.

Alternatively, if he opens a 12-14 HCP 1NT you should pass with:

♠ Q 8 4   ♡ A 7 5   ◇ Q 8 5 2   ♣ K 6 2

Even if you have a combined 25 HCP, game is likely to be a doubtful proposition with your isolated honours, non-existent intermediate cards, and lack of a good suit to attack. Replace the ♣ K with the ♣ A and there would still be a case for passing, if your nerves are strong enough!

In duplicate pairs, finding the highest-scoring denomination takes priority over bidding borderline games.

Fits and misfits

West	East
♠ 6	♠ A Q 4 3 2
♡ A Q 8 7 5 3	♡ 6
◇ K Q 8	◇ 9 6 4 3
♣ J 9 2	♣ K 10 8

Suppose you open the above West hand 1♡ and your 2♡ rebid over partner's 1♠ response is passed out. Hearts break 4-2 with the ♡ K lying offside and you only escape for one off because the ♣ Q lies well. Your initial reaction to your vulnerable score of −100 may be one of disappointment, cursing your misfit and the bad break, but you will be pleasantly surprised when you open the travelling score slip. It is unlikely that a single East/West pair will have recorded a positive score, and a good proportion of them will have conceded anything from −200 (3♡-2 or 2NT-2) to −400 (3NT-4). Such a misfit is a golden opportunity for the player with good judgement to score well, as the ability to escape with a small minus with misfitting hands is the mark of the expert. East earned your top by passing 2♡, rather than chasing rainbows with 2♠ or 2NT. He had good reasons to pass, apart from the obvious one of having a weak hand. Firstly your 2♡ rebid consumed so much space that a six-card suit was very likely. Secondly, he could not see a source of tricks without using your trump suit. Thirdly, if he passed there was always a chance that North/South would protect and get into trouble.

Incidentally, this hand demonstrates again why it can be dangerous to protect if opponents have not found a fit.

After the same start to the auction, 2♠ would be a reasonable bid with hand a), or with b), because an obvious source of tricks is available.

a) ♠ Q J 10 8 7 4   ♡ 2   ◇ 9 6 4   ♣ Q 10 8
b) ♠ K Q J 10 9   ♡ —   ◇ 10 9 8 4   ♣ K 10 9 8

Of course, if you find a fit the opposite reasoning applies. In the uncontested auction you must be positive, and in the competitive auction you must strain to announce your fit, even at the expense of bidding one level higher than you would like.

Sacrificing

Consider your action at *Green* vulnerability with this hand after the sequence below:

♠ 9 6 4 3   ♡ 7 4   ◇ 8 5 2   ♣ Q J 7 4

South	West	North	East
1♡	1♠	3♡	No
4♡	No	No	?

You can see no reason to believe that 4♡ will be defeated, but even at favourable vulnerability 4♠ could be expensive. If you sacrifice at teams of four the best you are likely to achieve is to turn −620 into −500, hardly worth the trouble! However, such a sacrifice at duplicate pairs could give you a top score! The issue would be clearcut; −500 would be a triumph whereas −800 (four off) would be a disaster! It would not be easy for North/South to hold you to six tricks when you have at least a nine-card fit; and they know it, making it likely that they will bid on to 5♡ rather than double. This might even give you a chance of beating them!

Sacrificing at pairs is often balancing on a knife-edge as one trick difference can transform a clear top into a cold bottom. To sacrifice you must not only be confident that the enemy contract is likely to make, but also believe that the rest of the room will bid it. If they have bid hesitantly to game, or you have pushed them into it, even a cheap sacrifice may only give you a few match-points so it is better to take your chance of defeating them. Equally, it is rarely good tactics to save against your opponents' slam unless you believe your sacrifice will cost less than their *game*, because it is likely that many pairs will not bid the slam.

Note that if you do succeed in pushing North/South into 5♡, partner will spoil all your good work if he sacrifices further, or doubles. If you have succeeded in pushing them into an unmake-able contract you will score well without doubling. On the other hand 5♡ doubled and making will earn you a dreadful score.

More on doubling

Generally speaking a double of a freely-bid contract carries the same message as it would at rubber bridge, namely lead-directing. In particular, if you double a slam you are demanding an *unusual* lead, often dummy's first side suit rather than the unbid suit. This is called a *Lightner* double. The message is often that you can ruff the opening lead.

It is a fallacy to imagine that you should double just because you think they have bid to a stupid contract.

Suppose you, as West, hold hand a) after the following sequence:

South	West	North	East
1♡	No	3♡	No
4NT	No	5◇	No
6♡	?		

a) ♠ A 7 5   ♡ 9 7 5   ◇ A 9 4 3 2   ♣ 6 3

It is tempting to double, but pointless. The bidding does suggest that you can cash two aces, but in that case you will get a top whatever you do. If either North or South has a void a double will give you a round zero on the board.

The time to double is not when you suspect they have bid badly, but when they have bid correctly to a contract that will fail because you have an unpleasant surprise for them. In that case you can expect other pairs to duplicate their auction, and the increased penalty will be necessary to score well. Double with hand b) after auction i) and lead a spade. Not only do you hold the red suits sitting after South, but you have every reason to believe that East has a useful spade holding sitting over North. Since South is likely to have at most one spade, and North will have few, if any, outside entries, there is no serious risk that you will help declarer to establish dummy's suit.

i)	South	West	North	East	ii)	South	West	North	East
	1♡	No	1♠	No		1♠	No	2♠	No
	2♢	No	2♠	No		2NT	No	3♠	No
	2NT	?				No	?		

b)	♠ 8	♡ K J 9 7	♢ A Q 10 2	♣ K 9 4 2
c)	♠ K Q J 10	♡ 8	♢ 9 6 4 2	♣ 10 7 3 2

Equally, double with hand c) after auction ii). At teams you might be afraid of pushing your opponents into 3NT, but your main concern playing pairs is that all East/West pairs are likely to get a plus score because of the bad spade break. (East is marked with some values on the bidding.) Therefore you must maximise your plus to score well.

Note that when deciding on a double based on your knowledge of potential bad breaks and the position of honours, you need to distinguish between auctions in which both opponents are limited, making it clear that they have little to spare for their contract, and those in which one opponent is unlimited. With either i) or ii) it is plain that you and your partner have at least 16 combined points. Therefore you can imagine his points even if you can't see them! I would double after auction i) with as little as:

♠ 8　　♡ K J 9 3　　♢ Q 10 7 3　　♣ J 10 9 8

You have a safe opening lead (the ♣ J), every finesse declarer takes is likely to fail, and two or three off is by no means unlikely. But be very wary of sequence iii):

iii) | South | West | North | East |
|---|---|---|---|
| 1♠ | No | 3♠ | No |
| 4♠ | ? | | |

North is limited, but all you can tell about South is that he doesn't fancy a slam. If you double with a hand like c) you might find declarer makes his game by brute force, losing only three trump tricks. If you are desperate for a top by all means double, but that is a calculated risk!

Quiz

1) Your partner opens 1NT and your right-hand opponent passes. What do you respond with these hands?

a)	♠ K Q	♡ A K J	◇ Q 4 3 2	♣ A 5 3 2
b)	♠ K Q	♡ A K J	◇ 6 4 3 2	♣ 7 5 3 2
c)	♠ 9 5	♡ A 9	◇ 8 3 2	♣ A K 10 9 6 3
d)	♠ A K Q	♡ 8 3 2	◇ Q 8 3	♣ 8 6 3 2

2) Your partner opens 1♡ and responds 2◇ over your 1♠ response. What is your second bid with these hands?

a)	♠ J 7 5 4 3 2	♡ K 7	◇ Q 2	♣ 8 4 2
b)	♠ K Q J 10 9	♡ 9 4	◇ 9 4 2	♣ 8 4 2
c)	♠ K Q 7 4 3	♡ 6	◇ 8 3	♣ A K 6 3 2

3) In which of these auctions has the bidding shown that *both* opponents have nothing to spare? Which bids give you the necessary information?

i) West	East		ii) West	East		iii) West	East
1NT	3♣		1♠	2♠		1◇	3◇
3NT			3◇	4♠		3NT	

iv) West	East		v) West	East		vi) West	East
1♡	1♠		1NT	2♣		1◇	1♠
2♣	2NT		2♡	3♡		2◇	2♠
3NT			4♡			2NT	

vii) West	East		viii) West	East		ix) West	East
1♠	3♠		1♡	2♡		1♡	2♣
4♠			2NT	3♡		2♡	3♡
						4♡	

4) Which of these hands is worth a double:
 i) As East after sequence i).
 ii) As West after sequence ii).
 iii) Whether or not you double as West, what would you
 lead?

i)	South	West	North	East		ii)	South	West	North	East
	1◇	No	1♠	No			1◇	No	1♠	No
	2♣	No	2♠	No			2♣	No	2♠	No
	2NT	No	3NT	?			2NT	No	3NT	No
							No	?		

a)	♠ A K Q	♡ 9 6 3	◇ K 7 4 2	♣ 9 4 2
b)	♠ A Q 10 9	♡ 7 4 3	◇ 9	♣ J 9 8 3 2
c)	♠ 7 2	♡ 9 5 3	◇ A J 9 8	♣ K J 8 7

Answers to quiz
1) a) 3NT. Don't be dazzled by your 19 HCP! Everything is
 wrong with this hand, and the chances of a good slam are
 minimal. In particular, you have no good intermediate
 cards, and your high cards are unattractively placed in
 your *short* suits. This is just the sort of hand where a strong
 pair earns a top by staying out of trouble while the whole
 room fails in a 33 HCP slam.
 b) 2NT. Again a discerning evaluation of this hand would
 treat it as nearer 12 HCP than 13.
 c) 3NT. This time you have a good source of tricks, your
 attractive club suit.
 d) Pass. Clearcut! Look at it like this. If you pass 1NT one
 bad thing might happen, the rest of the room bids a thin
 3NT and the cards lie well. On the other hand if you bid on
 there are *two* disagreeable outcomes. Either partner
 might be minimum and fail in 2NT, or he might be
 maximum and fail in 3NT.

2) a) 2♡. Partner's sequence promises at least 5 hearts. Your
 spades are too weak to repeat.
 b) 2♠. This time you have one less spade, but look at the
 difference in quality! This suit would play well opposite a
 singleton. Indeed, unless spades are trumps there will be
 no entries to your hand if partner *has* got a singleton.

c) 2NT. The argument 'He has the red suits and I have the blacks. We both have an opening bid so 3NT is correct' is a fallacy. No trumps may indeed be best, but prefer to underbid with a misfit. The hand won't play well because of severe communication problems. If partner cannot summon up the third no trump you are quite high enough!

3)   i) West is limited by his 1NT opening bid but East is unlimited. All you know is that he doesn't fancy a slam.
ii) East is limited by his 2♠. West is limited by his failure to bid game directly without a trial bid.
iii) East is limited by his 3◇, but West could have 19 HCP!
iv) West is limited by his inability to raise to more than 2♠. East is limited by bidding only 2NT on the second round.
v) West is limited by his 1NT opening, and East is limited by his failure to raise to more than 3♡.
vi) Both are limited by their second round bids, indeed it is difficult to imagine West's 2NT bid as being other than grossly undisciplined!
vii) East is limited by only raising to 3♠, but West is unlimited and could have a lot to spare.
viii) West is limited by only bidding 2NT, and East by his failure to bid game.
ix) West is limited by his 2♡ rebid, and East by his inability to bid game without further help.
     Therefore, if you have reason to believe that the distribution is going to be particularly unkind to declarer, chance a double after auctions ii), iv), v), vi), viii), and ix), but only double after i), iii) and vii) if you can defeat the contract by yourself. Even then, beware of declarer running to a safer haven, for example 4◇ after auction iii).

4) These bidding sequences ask for a double if you have an unpleasant surprise for declarer. North is limited by his 2♠ rebid, and South by his inability to jump on the second bid or bid more than 2NT third time.
a) i) and ii) You have no reason to double as East or West. Your ♠ A K Q may look impressive but you have no *surprises* for declarer. He is almost certainly expecting to

make his contract without dummy's spades, and you will probably make your spades, the ♢ K, and nothing else!

iii) As West lead a passive heart, or perhaps the ♠ A.

b) i) Double as East. Your spades are hovering menacingly over dummy's suit, and neither minor suit is breaking for declarer. Also you would welcome a spade lead rather than a fourth-highest heart which is likely to cost a trick.

ii) As West you shouldn't double, although the bad minor suit breaks are likely to inconvenience declarer.

iii) Lead a passive heart as West.

c) i) As East it looks as if every finesse is working for declarer, so pass.

ii) Double as West. You have the diamonds and clubs sitting over declarer, and no doubt partner has the spades sitting over dummy. This could be a bloodbath.

iii) As West lead a passive heart again, East's spades can wait!

Part 2   Bidding Conventions

5. Your Choice of System

Bridge systems can be divided into two categories.

Firstly, there are systems in which the opening bid seeks to suggest a denomination. Acol is an obvious example of such a natural system, with the game-forcing 2♣ as the only common conventional opening bid.

Secondly, there are the systems in which your first responsibility is to announce your strength. The fundamental principle underpinning the strong club systems is that all hands with 17 or more points are opened 1♣ (or perhaps with a two-level bid like 2NT). Often, as with Precision Club, they weld on additional requirements for opening 1♡ or 1♠, usually a five-card suit. An inevitable consequence is that the 1◇ opening also has to be semi-artificial, guaranteeing no more than two diamonds.

The attraction of the artificial systems is that a game-forcing sequence can be established very cheaply, giving plenty of bidding space to investigate the best contract. Given a clear run, a strong Precision pair will expect to bid at slam level more accurately than an Acol pair. However, opponents have been quick to realise that much of the increased accuracy of Precision asking-bids can be negated if they pre-empt violently. The Precision Club player who is dealt an Acol two-bid in hearts may be happy to start with 1♣, intending to show his suit on the next round, but he will be rather less happy if his non-vulnerable left-hand opponent leaps to 4♠ and his partner doubles or passes. His partner would have had a much better chance of making a successful decision if he knew opener's suit!

On the other hand, the strength of a natural system like Acol is that it is easier to bid accurately in the part-score zone, when an inability to be sure whether or not your partner's suit is genuine is a crippling handicap if your opponents quickly find a fit.

Not surprisingly, in the dog fight of duplicate pairs bidding where the part-score hand carries as many match-points as the slam hand, where asking bids too often inform defenders how to prevent overtricks, and where aggressive pre-emptive bidding is the order of the day, I would unhesitatingly recommend Acol, or Benjaminised Acol.

BENJAMINISED ACOL

This popular variation of Acol aims to shunt all the hands that would merit an Acol two-level opening into just three bids: 2♣, 2◇, and 2NT. This frees 2♡ and 2♠ for pre-emptive purposes. Undoubtedly having to open strong hands with an artificial bid does leave you vulnerable to the same nuisance bidding that plagues the Precision clubbers, but this is more than compensated for by the frequency of occurrence of the weak two pre-emptive bids.

The Benjamin 2◇ opening

This bid is game-forcing, showing a hand that would be worth an Acol 2♣ opening. The negative response is 2♡ (just as 2◇ is the negative response to 2♣). If opener rebids a suit it is economical to use the next bid up as a second negative (called a *Herbert* negative), showing 0-3 HCP.

The Benjamin 2♣ opening

This bid shows an *Acol Two*-bid in an unspecified suit. The negative response is 2◇ and a suit rebid is forcing for one round, just like an Acol two opening. The advantage of using 2♣ rather than 2◇ to open the slightly weaker 'strong' hands is that it is more likely that opener's suit can be shown at the two level. Indeed, after 2♣ No 2◇ No 2♡ responder is at an *advantage* compared to Acol because he has already shown 0-7 HCP. Therefore he can cheaply distinguish between the total bankruptcy of 0-3 HCP which he shows with a second (*Herbert*) negative bid of 2♠, and slightly more encouraging other rebids (4-7 HCP and game-forcing). Note that by partnership agreement, 2NT over a 2♡ rebid can conventionally show 4-7 HCP and a spade suit.

Of course there is inevitably one area of loss. You now cannot show an Acol two-bid in *either* minor below the three level. Therefore, faced with a hand that gives you a borderline decision between opening a minor suit at the one level or 2♣, prefer the one level opening bid.

Strong, balanced hands

With 20-22 HCP open 2NT.

With 23-24 HCP open 2♣ and rebid a non-forcing 2NT over the negative 2◇ response. If responder decided to bid on, the structure of bidding is the same as over a 2NT opening. You will find more on this in chapter 7.

With 25-26 HCP open 2◇ and rebid a game-forcing 2NT over a 2♡ negative response. Again the continuations should be the same as over a 2NT opening bid.

With 27-28 HCP open 2♣ and rebid a non-forcing 3NT. 4♣ then asks opener to start bidding four-card suits in ascending order.

With 29-30 HCP open 2◇ and rebid a non-forcing 3NT. The 4♣ continuation is as above.

Weak two opening bids (2♡ and 2♠)

2♡ shows 6-10 HCP and six *good* hearts. As with all pre-emptive bids, your HCP should be concentrated in your suit. At love all open 2♡ with a), but pass with b); Hand c) would be a reasonable 2♡ opening at RED vulnerability when you are justifiably wary of the dangers of opening 3♡. You should not open with a weak two-bid (or any other pre-empt) with four cards in the other major, so pass with d).

a) ♠ K 4	♡ A Q 10 7 5 2	◇ 9 4 3	♣ 7 2
b) ♠ K J 5	♡ Q 8 5 4 3 2	◇ K 9 3	♣ 4
c) ♠ 7	♡ K J 9 7 6 4 3	◇ A 8 3	♣ 9 2
d) ♠ Q 10 6 3	♡ A Q 10 7 5 2	◇ 9 7	♣ 3

If partner opens 2♡, a change of suit is natural and forcing, and 3NT is to play. Opener, having shown his hand-type with his 2♡ opening bid, should *never* remove to 4♡!

A raise to 3♡ is pre-emptive, *not* requesting opener to climb to 4♡ with a maximum 2♡ opening.

If responder wants more information before deciding between part-score or game (or between game and slam) he can request clarification from opener by using the conventional 2NT response. This confirms opener's suit as trumps and requests him to classify his hand as follows:

Good suit = two of the top three honours.
Maximum opening = good 8, to 10 HCP.

Opener then rebids as follows:

    3♣ = Poor suit, minimum opening.
    3◇ = Good suit, minimum opening.
    3♡ = Poor suit, maximum opening.
    3♠ = Good suit, maximum opening.

Quiz

1) Playing Benjaminised Acol at *Love all*, what do you open with these hands? If your opening is a *strong* two-level bid give your rebid over the conventional negative response, and say whether this rebid is not forcing, forcing for one round, or game-forcing.

a)	♠ A K J 7 4	♡ A Q J 6	◇ A K Q	♣ 4
b)	♠ A Q J 8 7 4	♡ A 7	◇ A Q J 2	♣ 4
c)	♠ 4	♡ A 7	◇ A Q J 2	♣ A Q J 8 7 4
d)	♠ A Q 7 4	♡ A Q J	◇ Q 10	♣ A K Q 7
e)	♠ A Q 7 4	♡ A Q J	◇ A 10	♣ A K Q 7
f)	♠ A K J 4	♡ A Q J	◇ A 10	♣ A K Q 7
g)	♠ Q 8 7 4 2	♡ A K Q 6	◇ A K Q	♣ 4
h)	♠ A J 10 8 6 3	♡ 9 5	◇ 9	♣ K 8 4 3
i)	♠ A J 10 8 6 3	♡ K 8 4 3	◇ 9	♣ 9 5

2) For the two North hands below, decide your rebid at *Game all* after each of these bidding sequences.

	i) South	North	ii) South	North	iii) South	North
	2◇	2♡	2◇	2♡	2♣	2◇
	2♠	?	2NT	?	2NT	?

a)	♠ 9 6	♡ K 8 5 3 2	◇ 7 2	♣ 9 7 4 3
b)	♠ 8 4	♡ Q 7 5 3	◇ 9 6 3	♣ K 6 4 2

3) What do you respond to your partner's weak 2♡ opening bid with these hands at *Love all*:

a) ♠ 6 3   ♡ K Q 5   ◇ A J 6 2   ♣ 9 5 3 2
b) ♠ 6   ♡ K Q 5 2   ◇ A J 6 2   ♣ 9 5 3 2
c) ♠ K J 2   ♡ Q 3   ◇ A Q 6 2   ♣ A K 3 2
d) ♠ K J 2   ♡ Q 3   ◇ A Q 6 2   ♣ A 8 3 2
e) ♠ K J 3   ♡ 8   ◇ A Q 8 2   ♣ K 6 5 3 2
f) ♠ K Q 8 6 4 3 ♡ 7   ◇ A K 8 4   ♣ A 3
g) ♠ K 5   ♡ 7   ◇ A K Q 8 6 5 2 ♣ K Q 10

Answers to quiz

1) a) Open 2◇ and rebid a game-forcing 2♠ over 2♡.
   b) Open 2♣ and rebid 2♠, forcing for one round, over 2◇.
   c) Open 1♣. Your hand would be just about worth an Acol two-bid in clubs if you could show your suit at the two-level. However the need to make a forcing rebid at the *three*-level after a 2◇ negative response is not attractive. Add the ♡ Q and a 2♣ opening would be justified.
   d) Open 2♣, and rebid a non-forcing 2NT over 2◇.
   e) Open 2◇, and rebid a game-forcing 2NT over 2♡.
   f) Open 2♣, and rebid a non-forcing 3NT over 2◇.
   g) Open 1♠. Your spades are not strong enough for an Acol two opening bid, or the Benjaminised 2♣ equivalent.
   h) Open 2♠, showing 6-10 HCP and six spades.
   i) Pass. Don't open a weak two-bid with four cards in the other major suit.

2) a) i) 2NT, a *Herbert* negative, showing 0-3 HCP.
      ii) and iii) 3♡. Game-forcing, as it would be over a 2NT opening bid. (3◇ if you play transfers. *See* chapter 7.)
   b) i) 3♣. The best available bid. 3NT is a possible alternative but it would then be difficult to find a 4-4 heart fit. 2NT is *not* an alternative because it is conventional – 0-3 HCP.
      ii) and iii) 3♣. Stayman (or Baron). Again see chapter 7 for a more advanced treatment.

3) a) 3♡. Mildly pre-emptive, attempting to dissuade opponents from seeking their spade fit.
   b) 4♡. Even more pre-emptive. It is even possible that you can make 4♡ *and* your opponents can make 4♠.
   c) 4♡. This time expecting to make by brute strength, and

woe betide any opponent who dares to compete! Thus if you jump to 4♡ nobody knows whether you have b) or c)! This doesn't concern your partner as he is expected to pass, but it is a major problem for your opponents who are forced to guess whether you are swindling them out of a laydown game, or ready to wield the axe if they venture into the auction.

d) 2NT. If opener shows a maximum 2♡ opening with 3♡ or 3♠ you will convert to 4♡. Otherwise sign off in 3♡.

c) Pass. Go quietly with a misfit! 2NT will *not* be better because you have no source of tricks without your partner's heart suit. This hand demonstrates why it is efficient to use 2NT as a conventional asking-bid. It is very rarely needed as a natural bid!

f) 2♠. Natural and forcing.

g) 3NT. To play. Opener will *never* bid 4♡, having already described his assets with his pre-empt.

6. The Crowhurst Convention

Playing duplicate bridge, most pairs choose the weak no trump. They accept the occasional adverse penalty (which, after all, is only one bottom as compared to a potential major disaster at rubber bridge) in order to gain the advantages listed below.

i) You tend to get to the correct contract quicker after a 1NT opening bid, with the great advantage of not revealing the most profitable line of defence! A weak no trump occurs more frequently than a strong no trump, hence it is efficient to use this convenient bid as often as possible.

ii) 1NT has considerable pre-emptive effect. It can sometimes be difficult for opponents to enter the bidding when the contract rightly belongs to them. Even if 1NT fails it often gives you an excellent score if opponents can score 110 or 140 in a major suit contract.

iii) Using a weak no trump you never need to open a prepared
1♣. In the highly competitive part-score auctions that develop at
duplicate pairs it is important to be able to raise partner's suit
without worrying whether it is real!

However there is also a *disadvantage* to the weak no trump.
Because the no-trump rebids occupy the point range between the
12-14 1NT opening bid, and the 20-22 HCP 2NT, with a 12-14
HCP hand you must either open 1NT or lose the chance to bid no
trumps. In practice you have to start almost all balanced 12-14
HCP hands with 1NT, otherwise you have no rebid. Sometimes
you then find that you have a good eight-card major fit that would
have scored better than 1NT, but as responder was too weak to
use Stayman it was never found.

A very popular attempt to improve on this is to redesign the
1NT rebid to cover the range 12-16 HCP. The 2♣ continuation
(called the *Crowhurst* convention) is artificial, asking about
opener's point count and simultaneously investigating a major
suit fit. The principle is that opener replies with a bid below 2NT
if he has 12-13 HCP, bids 2NT with 14 HCP, and jumps to the
three-level with 15-16 HCP. He also tries to show his lowest
undisclosed major suit feature (e.g. a fifth heart if he opened 1♡,
an unbid four-card heart suit, or three cards in responder's major
suit). With no feature to show he replies with a conventional
diamond bid, following the same principle as Stayman. If he has
two features to show he starts with the lower. For example:

Opener	Responder
1♣	1♠
1NT	2♣ (Crowhurst convention)
?	

2♢ = 12-13 HCP, not 4 hearts or 3 spades.
2♡ = 12-13 HCP, with 4 hearts, perhaps also 3 spades.
2♠ = 12-13 HCP, with 3 spades but not 4 hearts.
2NT = 14 HCP. Responder can enquire further with 3♣.
3♢ = 15-16 HCP, not 4 hearts or 3 spades.
3♡ = 15-16 HCP, with 4 hearts, perhaps also 3 spades.
3♠ = 15-16 HCP, with 3 spades but not 4 hearts.

For his Crowhurst 2♣ responder must have at least 10 HCP, as
he may be forced to play in 2NT if opener has only 12. This

highlights the disadvantage of such a wide-ranging no-trump rebid, as responder must explore game with 10 HCP in case opener has 16 HCP. Nevertheless, the advantages comfortably outweigh the drawbacks.

After the Crowhurst 2♣, a jump by either player should be played as game-forcing.

i) West	East	ii) West	East	iii) West	East
1♣	1♠	1♣	1♠	1♣	1♠
1NT	2♣	1NT	2♣	1NT	2♣
3♡	3♠	2♡	3♠	2NT	3♣
				3♡	3♠

In auction i) 3♡ is game-forcing. 3♠ shows five spades.

In auction ii) 3♠ is game-forcing. If after 2♡ East had continued with just 2♠ that would have been a sign-off.

In auction iii) 2NT shows exactly 14 HCP, but gives no information on suit length. East could have passed this, but once he chooses to continue with 3♣ asking for West's lowest major feature, that should also be game-forcing. As in i) West has four hearts and East has five spades.

This convention gives you an alternative to opening 1NT with some 12-14 HCP balanced hands, but before committing yourself check that responder cannot embarrass you by changing suit at the two-level.

a)	♠ 9 8	♡ A J 7 4	◇ K 8 2	♣ K Q 9 6
b)	♠ K Q 9 6	♡ K 8 2	◇ A J 7 4	♣ 9 8
c)	♠ J 9	♡ K 9 4 3 2	◇ A Q 8	♣ K 4 2

With a) you can open 1♣, intending a 1♡ rebid over 1◇, or 1NT over 1♠. However with b) either 1♠ or 1◇ would leave you without a rebid if the response is 2♣, so you must open 1NT. With c) open 1♡, intending to rebid 2♡ over 2♣ or 2◇, but delighted to rebid a 12-16 1NT over a 1♠ response.

The wide-range 1NT protective overcall

A 1NT overcall in the protective position has traditionally shown 11-14 HCP, but this leaves far too many balanced hands with more than 14 HCP for the available sequences. The modern adaptation is to play the protective 1NT as showing 11-16 HCP, with a Crowhurst enquiry bid available for partner. The 1NT overcaller replies to 2♣ as follows:

2◇ = 11-13 HCP, not 4 hearts or 4 spades.
2♡ = 11-13 HCP, with 4 hearts, perhaps also 4 spades.
2♠ = 11-13 HCP, with 4 spades but not 4 hearts.
2NT = 14-16 HCP and game-forcing. Partner can enquire further with 3♣.

Quiz

1) With each of these hands you respond 1♡ to your partner's 1◇ opening bid. What is your next call if he rebids 1NT (showing 12-16 HCP)? If you decide to bid 2♣ consider your continuation over every possible rebid.

a)	♠ K J 6 4	♡ K 7 5 2	◇ A 2	♣ K 7 4
b)	♠ 7 3 2	♡ K J 9 7 5	◇ 8 2	♣ K 7 4
c)	♠ 7 3 2	♡ K J 9 7 5	◇ A 2	♣ K 7 4
d)	♠ K 3 2	♡ K J 9 7 5	◇ A 2	♣ K 7 4

2) With each of these hands you open 1♡ and rebid 1NT over 1♠. What is your third bid if responder continues with 2♣?

a)	♠ Q 8	♡ K Q 7 4 2	◇ A J 7	♣ J 7 3
b)	♠ Q 8	♡ K Q 7 4 2	◇ A J 7	♣ Q 7 3
c)	♠ Q 8	♡ K Q 7 4 2	◇ A J 7	♣ K 7 3
d)	♠ Q 8	♡ A K 7 4	◇ A J 7 2	♣ J 7 3
e)	♠ Q 8 2	♡ K Q 7 4	◇ A J 7	♣ K 7 3

3) With the hand below you respond 1♠ to your partner's 1♣ opening bid, and continue with 2♣ over his 1NT rebid. How do you proceed if his third bid is:

i) 2◇	ii) 2♡	iii) 2♠	iv) 2NT
v) 3◇	vi) 3♡	vii) 3♠	

♠ K J 6 4 2   ♡ Q 4   ◇ A 10 3   ♣ 7 6 2

4) All of these balanced hands are in the range 12-14 HCP. Decide your opening bid, and if you open with a suit bid give your rebid over each possible change of suit response.

a) ♠ A Q 7 4   ♡ 8 5   ◇ A K 7 2   ♣ 9 6 2
b) ♠ A Q 7 4   ♡ 8 5 2   ◇ A K 7 2   ♣ 9 6
c) ♠ 10 5   ♡ A Q 7 4   ◇ 8 5 2   ♣ A K 7 2
d) ♠ 10 5   ♡ 8 5 2   ◇ A Q 7 4   ♣ A K 7 2

Answers to quiz

1) a) 3NT. 2♣ is a waste of time as his 1NT rebid denies 4 hearts or 4 spades.
   b) Pass. It is not wise to sign off in a five-card suit because partner's shape could even be 3-1-5-4.
   c) 2♣. Convert 2◇ to 2NT, pass 2♡, enquire with 3♣ over 2NT, convert 3◇ to 3NT, or raise 3♡ to 4♡.
   d) 2♣. Bid 3NT over 2◇ or 3◇, raise 2♡ or 3♡ to 4♡, and continue with 3♣ over 2NT.

2) a) 2♡, showing 12-13 HCP and 5 hearts.
   b) 2NT, showing 14 HCP and nothing about your shape.
   c) 3♡, showing 15-16 HCP and 5 hearts. You are not necessarily denying 3 spades.
   d) 3◇, showing 15-16 HCP, but not 5 hearts or 3 spades.
   e) 3♠, showing 15-16 HCP and 3 spades, but not 5 hearts.

3)   i) 2NT. A sign-off.
   ii) 2♠. It is still possible that partner has three-card spade support. He will convert to 2NT if totally unsuitable for a spade contract.
   iii) Pass. You have no game ambitions opposite 12-13 HCP.
   iv) Pass. Partner has 14 HCP so it is reasonable to stay out of game at pairs.
   v) 3NT. Partner has denied 3 spades.
   vi) 3♠. Partner will raise to 4♠ with 3 spades, or convert to 3NT with only a doubleton in your suit.
   vii) 4♠. The obvious contract.

4) a) Open 1NT. After either 1◇ or 1♠ you have no good rebid over 2♣. (Note that the sequence 1♠ No 2♣ No 2◇ shows 5 spades.)
   b) Open 1NT, for the same reason as a).
   c) Open 1♣. Rebid 1♡ over 1◇, raise 1♡ to 2♡, or rebid 1NT over 1♠.
   d) Open 1♣. Raise 1◇ to 2◇, or rebid 1NT over 1♡ or 1♠.

7. Transfer Bidding

There are few conventional themes that have had such a wholly beneficial effect on the standard of bidding as transfer bids. The principle is that you bid the suit *below* your suit, forcing partner to bid your suit. Almost all serious pairs now play transfers when partner opens 1NT. There are two main advantages.

Firstly, it increases the probability that the 1NT bidder is declarer. More likely than not, his is the hand with the vulnerable tenaces that need protecting from the opening lead. It is also quite likely that his is the stronger hand, and it tends to be more difficult to defend accurately when the stronger hand is concealed.

Secondly, transfer bids multiply the number of sequences available, leading to greater definition. Using standard methods a 2♢ response to 1NT has just one meaning, a sign off. Using transfers this same 2♢ bid compels opener to rebid 2♡, and opens up a whole range of continuations.

The 2♢ response to 1NT

As stated above this compels opener to rebid 2♡. You would introduce any of these hands in this way.

a) ♠ 9 6	♡ K 7 5 4 3 2	♢ 9 6 4	♣ 7 2
b) ♠ 10	♡ K J 7 6 3	♢ A 10 9 7	♣ 8 7 3
c) ♠ 8 2	♡ Q 9 7 4 3 2	♢ A K	♣ J 5 2
d) ♠ 8 2	♡ Q 9 7 4 3 2	♢ A K	♣ A 5 2
e) ♠ 8 2	♡ K Q 8 5 3	♢ A 8 5	♣ Q 10 8
f) ♠ K 2	♡ K Q 8 5 3	♢ A 8 5	♣ Q 10 8
g) ♠ A K J 4	♡ A Q 8 5 3	♢ Q 6 3	♣ 7
h) ♠ 7	♡ A Q 8 5 3	♢ Q 6 3	♣ A K J 4

With a), b), c), or d) you have decided that hearts will be the final denomination. Holding a) or b) you will pass 2♡, using the transfer as a sign-off. Holding c) you will raise 2♡ to 3♡, a game try. Since you have already shown five hearts the raise to 3♡ (rather than 2NT) shows a six-card suit. With d) you will jump to 4♡, the obvious contract.

With e), f), g), or h) you are using the transfer to inform opener that you have five hearts before suggesting another denomination. Holding e) you will continue with 2NT, showing exactly five hearts and enough to invite game. Partner will decide between final contracts of 2NT, 3♡, 3NT and 4♡. Note the advantage over traditional methods, where you can only make a game try with five hearts by starting with a Stayman 2♣ and jumping to 3♡ over 2◇. That is a bit high if 2NT is the best contract! With f) your second bid will be 3NT, inviting partner to correct to 4♡ if he has three-card support.

With g) and h) you will continue with your second suit, 2♠ and 3♣ respectively. 2♠ is forcing for one round, while it is best to play 3♣ as game-forcing, allowing opener to give preference to 3♠ even if maximum, and thus giving an extra round of bidding for slam exploration if responder is very strong. Hand h) illustrates the superiority of transfer bidding, as otherwise it would be impossible to show both suits without by-passing 3NT. Traditional responses to 1NT are not very efficient at showing two-suited hands!

The 2♡ response to 1NT

It won't surprise you that this bid requires opener to transfer to 2♠. The structure of continuations is similar to that outlined above.

Although the transfer virtually *demands* that opener bids 2♠, occasionally the knowledge that his partner has five spades may unearth such an outstanding fit that opener is justified in making an unsolicited game try. Suppose partner responds 2♡ to your 1NT opening, and you hold:

♠ K Q 7 4   ♡ A 6 2   ◇ A J 10 9   ♣ 9 2

You have at least a nine-card fit, good shape, and excellent control cards. Bid 3◇, agreeing spades and showing where your values lie. This may enable responder to bid game on minimal values if the hands fit well, for example with:

♠ A 8 6 3 2   ♡ 10 7   ◇ K Q 6 3   ♣ 10 8

If he is not interested in game he will sign off in 3♠, but even if that fails it is likely that your opponents can make 3♡ or 3♣ so you may score well. Your 3◇ bid is called *Breaking the Transfer*.

The 2♠ response to 1NT

Perhaps the best use for this bid is to seek out a 4-4 fit with a view to slam exploration. Thus responder should have at least 16 HCP and no five-card suit. Opener rebids 2NT with a minimum opening, otherwise he rebids his lowest four-card suit. Whatever the initial rebid, both players subsequently bid their four-card suits 'up the line' until a fit is found, or 3NT is reached. For example:

West	East	West	East
♠ A 8	♠ K J 4	1NT	2♠
♡ 10 7 5 3	♡ A 2	2NT (1)	3♣ (2)
◇ K Q 10 5	◇ A J 8 3	3◇ (2)	4◇ (3)
♣ K 7 4	♣ A Q 10 2	4♠ (4)	6◇ (5)

1) Showing a minimum 1NT opening.
2) Four-card suit.
3) A fit has been found.
4) Cue bid.
5) With only 31-32 combined HCP East doesn't expect 6NT to be a good contract.

Since opener is obliged to bid 2NT over a 2♠ response with a minimum opening bid, you can extend the use of 2♠ to include hands worth a 2NT *game try* over 1NT (i.e. 11-12 HCP without a four-card major.) You then pass a 2NT rebid, or convert a three level rebid to 3NT (which opener must pass). That frees a 2NT response for use as a transfer to 3♣, allowing you to sign off in clubs or diamonds. You will see the principle of a single bid catering for two (or more) vastly different meanings extended further when you meet the multi-coloured 2◇ opening bid in chapter 11.

The 2♣ response to 1NT

You have already seen how transfer bidding makes it possible to show a five-card major and a secondary four-card suit below

3NT. However there is still a problem if you have a five-card minor and a four-card major. Suppose partner opens 1NT and you hold:

♠ K Q 5 3   ♡ 9   ◇ A 8 5   ♣ K Q 9 7 3

An immediate 3♣ will fail to find a 4-4 spade fit, as opener will rebid 3NT if he dislikes clubs. Alternatively, if you start with a Stayman 2♣ you cannot subsequently show your clubs because 3♣ would be a sign off. However, if you use 2NT as a transfer to 3♣ you no longer need this sequence as a sign off, so why not play that 2♣ followed by 3♣ is forcing?

West	East	West	East
♠ A 7	♠ K Q 3 2	1NT	2♣
♡ J 8 2	♡ 4	2◇	3♣ (1)
◇ K Q 7 4	◇ A J 2	3◇ (2)	3♠ (3)
♣ K 8 5 4	♣ A Q J 7 2	4♣ (4)	6♣ (5)

1) At least 5 clubs, and game-forcing.
2) Interested in clubs (otherwise he would have rebid 3NT) and showing good diamonds.
3) Good spades. With good hearts West can now retreat to the inevitable pairs contract of 3NT.
4) Plainly hearts will be a problem in 3NT.
5) Since partner has no wasted heart values this is likely to be a reasonable contract.

Sequences over a 2NT opening bid

It is becoming increasingly popular to use 3♣ as an initial request for a *five*-card major. Opener will not normally open 1NT with five hearts or spades, but because an Acol two sequence demands an excellent suit there are many hands where 2NT is correct. Opener rebids 2◇ without a five-card major, and then both pairs bid four-card suits in ascending order until a fit is found or 3NT is reached.

Here are two examples.

West	East		West	East
♠ K J 6 5 3	♠ Q 8 4		2NT	3♣ (1)
♡ A 9 3	♡ 8 4		3♠	4♠
♢ A Q 7	♢ K 9 5 2			
♣ A K	♣ 9 6 4 2			

1) Unless West has five spades East will settle for 3NT.

West	East		West	East
♠ K J 6 5	♠ Q 10 7 2		2NT	3♣ (1)
♡ A 9 3	♡ 8 4		3♢ (2)	3♠ (3)
♢ A Q 7	♢ K 9 5 2		4♠	
♣ A K 3	♣ 9 6 4			

1) This time East is equally interested in a 4-4 spade fit.
2) Denying five of either major.
3) Four-card spade suit.

Over 2NT a 3♢ response is a transfer to 3♡, and 3♡ is a transfer to 3♠. 3♠ shows exactly five spades and four hearts, a shape that otherwise could not be shown without by-passing 3NT.

Finally, there are two crucial points to agree with your partner before disaster strikes!

i) Do transfers still operate if opponents enter the auction with a double or bid? My advice is to abandon transfers, indeed even Stayman is best abandoned after a double as the priority is to escape into a five-card suit.

ii) Do you play transfers after a natural no-trump overcall? The usual answer is 'yes'.

Defending against transfer sequences

The principles outlined here are consistent with the *Lebensohl* principles of chapter 10, only simpler. After South opens 1NT, West passes, and North transfers with 2♡, East can double to show hearts or bid 2♠ (the Anchor suit) as a takeout 'double' of 2♠. If he wants to make a *penalty* double of 2♠ he passes, and doubles next time if appropriate.

Quiz

1) Playing Stayman and transfers, what is your rebid at *Love all* with the hand below after each of these sequences?

i)	West	East	ii)	West	East	iii)	West	East
	1NT	2♢		1NT	2♡		1NT	2♠
	?			?			?	

iv)	West	East	v)	South	West	North	East
	1NT	2NT		1NT	Double	2♡	No
	?			?			

♠ K J 8 3   ♡ A 6   ♢ 8 7 4 3   ♣ A Q 3

2) Plan your strategy at *Love all* with these hands if partner opens 1NT.

a)	♠ A Q 9 6 5	♡ 8 7	♢ K 8 6	♣ 9 4 2
b)	♠ A Q 9 6 5	♡ 8 7	♢ K 8 6	♣ A 4 2
c)	♠ A Q 9 6 5	♡ K 7 5 3	♢ A 2	♣ 9 6
d)	♠ A Q 9 6 5	♡ K 9 7 5 3	♢ 2	♣ K 6
e)	♠ A K J	♡ Q 7 5	♢ K Q 4	♣ Q 8 7 3
f)	♠ A Q 2	♡ A Q J 5	♢ K Q 6 3	♣ 9 5
g)	♠ A J 7 3	♡ A 6	♢ 9	♣ K 10 9 7 5 3
h)	♠ 9	♡ 9 6 2	♢ K Q 8 7 5 3	♣ 8 4 2

3) With the hands below you bid 2♡ in response to your partner's 1NT opening bid. How do you continue over his enforced 2♠ rebid?

a)	♠ A J 9 4 2	♡ Q 5	♢ 9 6 5 3	♣ A 5
b)	♠ A K 9 4 2	♡ Q 5	♢ 9 6 5 3	♣ A 5
c)	♠ A 10 9 4 3 2	♡ Q 5	♢ 6 5 3	♣ A 5
d)	♠ A J 9 4 3 2	♡ 8 5	♢ 6 5 3	♣ A K
e)	♠ A J 9 4 2	♡ Q 5	♢ A Q J 3	♣ 8 5
f)	♠ A J 9 4 2	♡ 8	♢ A J 9 4	♣ J 3 2

4) You open the hands below with 1NT and obediently transfer to 2♠ over partner's 2♡. For each hand state how you continue after these rebids:

i) 2NT   ii) 3♢   iii) 3♡   iv) 3♠   v) 3NT

a)   ♠ K 8 7   ♡ A 6   ♢ K 4 3 2   ♣ Q 10 4 3
b)   ♠ K 8 7   ♡ A 6   ♢ K Q 3 2   ♣ Q 10 4 3
c)   ♠ K 7   ♡ A 9 8   ♢ Q 10 3 2   ♣ K 10 4 3
d)   ♠ K 7   ♡ A 9 8   ♢ K Q 3 2   ♣ Q 10 4 3

5) You open these hands 1NT and partner responds 2♠. What is your rebid?
a)   ♠ K J 7 4   ♡ 9 6 2   ♢ A J 8 5   ♣ K 2
b)   ♠ K J 7 4   ♡ Q 6 2   ♢ A J 8 5   ♣ K 2

6) What do you respond to your partner's 2NT opening lead with these hands? Also plan your continuation.
a)   ♠ Q 9 6   ♡ K 6 2   ♢ 8 5   ♣ 10 7 5 4 3
b)   ♠ Q 9 6   ♡ K 6 3 2   ♢ 8 5   ♣ 10 7 5 4
c)   ♠ K J 7 5 4   ♡ 9 6   ♢ Q 8 6 4   ♣ 10 7
d)   ♠ K J 7 5 4   ♡ Q 8 6 4   ♢ 9 6   ♣ 10 7

Answers to quiz

1)   i) 2♡. As instructed.
     ii) 3♣. With such good spades and control cards you should break the transfer and show where your values lie.
     iii) 3♢, showing a maximum 1NT opening and 4 diamonds.
     iv) 3♣, as instructed. Partner is intending to pass, or sign off in 3♢.
     v) Pass. After the double 2♡ is *not* a transfer.

2)   a) Bid 2♡ and pass the 2♠ response.
     b) Bid 2♡ and continue with 3NT over 2♠.
     c) Bid 2♡ and continue with 3♡ over 2♠, showing at least 5 spades and 4 hearts. If opener then bids 3NT, pass!
     d) Bid 2♡ and continue with 4♡ over 2♠, giving partner a choice between 4♡ and 4♠.
     e) Bid 3NT, the obvious contract. There is no point in giving away information with 2♠ because you are not seriously looking for a slam!
     f) Bid 2♠. If partner by-passes 2NT, thereby showing a better than minimum 1NT, and you find a 4-4 red suit fit, a slam is likely. Even if a diamond fit is established either

player can use 4NT as a natural bid if he doesn't fancy a slam.

g) Bid 2♣. Then raise 2♠ to 4♠. After any other rebid continue with 3♣. If opener then rebids 3NT, accept his decision.

h) Bid 2NT, and sign off in 3◇ over partner's forced 3♣.

3) a) Bid 2NT, showing 11-12 HCP and 5 spades.

b) Bid 3NT, showing 13+ HCP and 5 spades.

c) Bid 3♠, a game try showing 6 spades.

d) Bid 4♠. The obvious contract.

e) Bid 3◇, forcing and showing at least 5 spades and 4 diamonds.

f) Bid 2NT. It looks revolting with your small singleton heart, but 3◇ is game-forcing, and 3♠ shows a sixth spade. Even transfers don't solve everything!

4) a) i) Sign off in 3♠.

ii) and iii) Show your three-card spade support with a forcing 3♠.

iv) 4♠. You have a minimum 1NT opening but the 6-3 spade fit and doubleton heart is worth an extra trick. Alternatively, pass is OK if you feel cautious.

v) 4♠. Choose the 5-3 major suit fit.

b) i) 4♠. Bid game in the eight-card fit.

ii) and iii) 3♠. Forcing. Again you have an eight-card fit.

iv) 4♠. Your 1NT opening was maximum.

v) 4♠. Choose the 5-3 fit.

c) i) Pass. Minimum 1NT and only 2 spades.

ii) 4◇. Don't forget partner also knows that 3NT scores higher than 5◇, so if he is interested in a diamond contract you should co-operate.

iii) 3NT. You don't have 3 spades or 4 hearts.

iv) Pass. You couldn't be less suitable!

v) Pass. Partner has only 5 spades.

d) i) 3NT. The obvious game.

ii) 4◇. As with c).

iii) 3NT. Again as with c).

iv) 4♠. You have only 2 spades but your 1NT was maximum. Partner has 6 spades.

v) Pass. As with c).

5) a) 2NT. Showing a minimum 1NT opening bid.
   b) 3◇. Showing a maximum 1NT opening bid and 4 diamonds. 3◇ also denies 4 clubs as you would otherwise start with your lowest suit.

6) a) 3♣. Asking partner if he has a *five*-card major. Raise 3♡ to 4♡, or 3♠ to 4♠. Rebid 3NT over 3◇.
   b) 3♣. This time rebid 3♡ over 3◇ and opener will raise to 4♡ with four. Raise 3♡ to 4♡ or 3♠ to 4♠.
   c) 3♡. Then 3NT over 3♠, showing exactly 5 spades.
   d) 3♠, showing 5 spades and 4 hearts.

8. Takeout Doubles

Traditionally a double was only for takeout if these two conditions were both satisfied:
   i) A suit bid below 3NT is doubled.
   ii) Partner has previously done no more than pass.
This left many penalty doubles that were rarely used, and not surprisingly experts started to realise that it would be more efficient to reallocate these doubles to indicate a desire to compete. The conventional uses described in this chapter are effective in any form of bridge, but doubly so at duplicate pairs where it is so important to compete aggressively in order to win the part score battle.

THE SPUTNIK (OR NEGATIVE) DOUBLE

South	West	North	*Love all*
1◇	1♠	?	

♠ 8 5 3   ♡ A 8 5 2   ◇ K 7   ♣ 8 4 3 2

If West had passed you, as North, would have had an easy 1♡

response but his pre-emptive 1♠ overcall has made life difficult. Playing rubber bridge you could justify passing, relying on partner to protect if strong, but in a duplicate event it is only too likely that East will raise the stakes with 2♠, or even 3♠, giving you an even harder problem on the next round. The solution is to double *for takeout*, a *Sputnik* double. Of course that means you cannot make a penalty double, but the conditions for making a one-level penalty double are so stringent (excellent trumps and a misfit with partner) that the gain far outweighs the loss on grounds of frequency of use. And you will later see that it is possible to recover the penalty double!

Sputnik doubles are now examined in detail.

i)	South	West	North	ii)	South	West	North
	1♢	1♠	Double		1♢	1♡	Double

A Sputnik double of a major suit overcall at the one level promises four cards in the other major, and opener will initially assume it shows 6-9 HCP (although North may Sputnik with a stronger hand, intending to reveal his true values later.) Thus North shows four hearts in auction i) and four spades in auction ii). Plainly there is less need for the Sputnik double in ii) because no major suit has been cut out by the overcall; however these new takeout doubles are so effective that it is efficient to utilise the overcall to increase your bidding accuracy. If North had chosen to prefer a forcing 1♠ to a Sputnik double in auction ii) he would have shown a five-card spade suit, or perhaps a very strong four-card suit if he had a hand in which no other denomination except spades seemed attractive, e.g.,

♠ A Q 10 9   ♡ 8 5 4 3   ♢ Q 3   ♣ 8 4 2

iii)	South	West	North	iv)	South	West	North
	1♣	1♢	Double		1♡	1♠	Double

In auction iii) there are two unbid majors, and North should have four cards in at least one of them. On the other hand iv) has no unbid major. North should either have both minors and sufficient tolerance for hearts to be content for South to rebid a five-card suit (a), or one minor and three-card heart support so he can retreat to 2♡ if South rebids the wrong minor (b).

a) ♠ 8 4 3   ♡ Q 6   ◇ K J 6 2   ♣ Q 10 6 4
b) ♠ 8 4 3   ♡ 9 6 2   ◇ K J 6   ♣ A J 7 4

Note that in each case North is *prepared* for South's rebid.

You must plainly agree with your partner how high to play Sputnik doubles. I would suggest up to, and including, 2♠ overcalls. Common sense dictates that the higher the overcall, the more North needs for his double, but since *being prepared* is paramount it would be counter-productive to dwell too much on points.

v) South	West	North	vi) South	West	North
1◇	2♣	Double	1◇	2♠	Double

For auction v) North's hand could be as weak as c) because he is happy to pass any rebid; despite having a higher point count, d) would be unsuitable because he is unprepared for 2◇; e) is suitable because he is strong enough to remove an unwelcome 2◇ rebid to 2NT.

c) ♠ A 8 6 4   ♡ Q 9 5 4   ◇ 10 6 5   ♣ 8 2
d) ♠ A 8 6 4   ♡ Q 9 5 4   ◇ 10   ♣ J 9 8 2
e) ♠ A 8 6 4   ♡ Q 9 5 4   ◇ 5   ♣ A J 4 3

Finally, with auction vi) North must be aware that he is forcing South to rebid at the three level, therefore he should have nine HCP, or equivalent playing strength.

Responding to a Sputnik double

If the double guarantees one particular suit, South makes the rebid he would have done if North had bid that suit. This should not normally be a problem if the overcall was at the one level because he should have a rebid prepared!

South	West	North	East
1♣	1♡	Double	No
?			

a) ♠ K Q 6 4   ♡ K 6   ◇ 9 4   ♣ A 10 5 3 2
b) ♠ K Q 6 4   ♡ A 6   ◇ K 4   ♣ A 10 5 3 2
c) ♠ A J 5   ♡ 8 5 2   ◇ Q 8 5   ♣ A K J 6

North's double shows four spades.

With a) South would have raised 1♠ to 2♠ if West had passed. Therefore he makes a minimum spade rebid now, 1♠.

With b) South would have jump-raised a 1♠ response to 3♠, so he jumps to 2♠.

The only time South will be stuck is if he intended a no-trump rebid, but hasn't got the mandatory guard in the enemy suit. With c) he should improvise with 1♠.

If North had doubled a two-level overcall he would not necessarily be guaranteeing a specific suit; he should be prepared for South to bid anything, so South should not be afraid to introduce a major suit.

The penalty double re-appears!

So what does North do if South's 1♣ opening is overcalled by West's 1♡ and he would like to make a penalty double? He passes! Thus his pass either shows a weak hand, or a penalty double. Unless from his own hand he can tell that North cannot have a penalty double *South mustn't allow 1♡ to be passed out*. To determine his right course of action he decides how he would have reacted if North *had* been able to make a penalty double. If he would have passed he should reopen with a double, allowing North to pass.

South	West	North	East
1♢	1♡	No	No
?			

a)	♠ K 7	♡ 9 2	♢ A Q 7 5 3	♣ K J 6 3
b)	♠ K Q 7 5 3	♡ —	♢ K Q 10 7 6 2	♣ 8 4
c)	♠ 9 5	♡ K J 10 6	♢ A Q J 8 5	♣ K 8

With a) South doubles. If North removes this *he must have a weak hand*.

With b) South is fairly sure that North does want to penalise 1♡, but with such a great discrepancy between his playing strength and defensive strength he does not wish to co-operate. However, he must not pass as North may be very strong. He rebids 1♠.

Finally, with c) South's hearts are so good that he knows North cannot want to make a penalty double. Now is the time to pass!

THE RESPONSIVE DOUBLE

To obtain a good penalty from a low-level contract you need to catch a player who has taken a calculated risk to enter the auction, only to find his partner with a misfitting, poor hand. Once your opponents have found a fit, and are freely raising their chosen suit at the two or three level, it is very rare that you will want to make a penalty double. Therefore in the sequence shown below, East's double is best played for *takeout*. It is called a *Responsive double* because he is responding to West's double with a double of his own. He might have hand a).

i)	South	West	North	East
	1♦	Double	2♦	Double

a)   ♠ K 7 4 3   ♡ Q 6 5 2   ♦ 9 4   ♣ Q 10 5

He wants to compete at the two level but feels that a 4-4 fit is more likely to be found if West chooses the suit. If North/South have found a minor suit fit a responsive double should guarantee four cards in each major. Change the ♡2 for the ♣2 and East should take the responsibility of choosing the denomination upon his own shoulders, and bid 2♠. If he wrongly passes the buck back to West, it is quite likely that his unfortunate partner will have 4-4 in the majors, and pick the wrong one! Note that the focus is again on finding the *major* fit, which not only scores better, but can outbid the enemy suit at the three level if they compete further.

If North/South agree a major suit there is only one unbid major and different principles apply.

ii)	South	West	North	East
	1♡	Double	2♡	Double

iii)	South	West	North	East
	1♠	Double	2♠	Double

In auction ii) East should prefer 2♠, 3♠, or 3♡ to double if he has four spades, therefore the responsive double *denies* four spades. Perhaps he has:

♠ K 10 5   ♡ 9 2   ♦ K 7 4 3   ♣ Q 6 4 2

Auction iii) is difficult in that, unlike i) and ii), East cannot introduce his major suit at the two level. This leaves him short of bidding options without taking the bidding dangerously high. There are a number of desirable uses for the responsive double, for example, denying four hearts and showing equal length in the minors. We must choose the purpose that best satisfies the duplicate scoring system, and that points towards looking for a heart fit. I suggest that you bid 3♡ as a purely competitive manoeuvre (b), and double with four hearts and values for a game try (c).

b) ♠ 9 2 ♡ K 6 3 2 ◇ K 8 3 ♣ Q J 3 2
c) ♠ 9 2 ♡ K 6 3 2 ◇ K 8 3 ♣ A J 3 2

THE UNASSUMING CUE BID

i)	South	West	North	East	ii)	South	West	North	East
1♡	1♠	No	2♠		1♡	1♠	No	2♡
			or 3♠					

Have you discussed with your partner the meanings of East's spade raise in auction i)? Is he trying to pre-empt North/South out of their dues with hand a), or is he making a genuine game try with hand b)?

a) ♠ K Q 7 4 ♡ 9 7 ◇ Q 10 9 6 ♣ 9 5 4
b) ♠ Q 8 4 ♡ 9 7 ◇ A Q J 4 ♣ K 10 9 2
c) ♠ Q 8 4 ♡ 9 7 ◇ A Q 7 4 ♣ K Q 10 9

It is normal to play all direct raises of an overcalled suit as pre-emptive, therefore East must cue bid opener's suit with b), as in auction ii). This use of the opponent's suit as a game try in partner's overcalled suit is called an *Unassuming Cue Bid*. It initially shows a hand that would be worth raising a 1♠ opening to 3♠ if 1♠ showed a five-card suit (as indeed the overcall does). West can reject the game try by rebidding 2♠ (the lowest legal bid in his suit) or accept it, by-passing 2♠.

With c) East will start with 2♡ and raise 2♠ to 3♠, giving West the message that he is genuinely keen to play in game unless West's overcall is the garbage that can sometimes justify a one-level duplicate pairs overcall.

THE COMPETITIVE DOUBLE

iii)	South	West	North	East	iv)	South	West	North	East
	1♡	1♠	2♡	Double		1♡	1♠	3♡	Double

Although this time West overcalled instead of doubled, North/South have again found a low-level fit so the same logic dictates that East's double should be for takeout. When space permits these *Competitive doubles* focus attention on the unbid suits. In auction iii) East could have made a 3♡ Unassuming Cue Bid if he wanted to agree spades and make a game try, therefore double shows hand a), with the minor suits and tolerance for spades.

a)   ♠ 8 2   ♡ 8 5 3   ◇ K J 7 3   ♣ A Q 3 2

Sometimes the bidding is too high for an Unassuming Cue Bid to allow East/West to stop short of game, for example in auction iv). In that case, on the grounds of frequency of use (the main priority is to distinguish between hands a) and b) on page 61). 3♠ is normally played as purely competitive, while double fulfils the game try function of the Unassuming Cue Bid.

Opener's side can also play competitive and responsive doubles. Consider these auctions:

v)	South	West	North	East	vi)	South	West	North	East
	1♡	1♠	2◇	2♠		1♡	1♠	Double	2♠
	Double					Double			

vii)	South	West	North	East
	1♡	2◇	2♡	3◇
	Double			

In each case East/West are raising their chosen suit, so South's double is for takeout. Perhaps he holds hand b) for auction v) and is happy for North to continue with 3♣, 3◇ or 3♡. Equally for auction vi) he probably holds hand c).

After auction vii) North/South have already found a fit so the denomination is not in doubt. 3♡ would be merely contesting the part-score, hand d), so double is used for a game try hand e).

b)	♠ 9 4	♡ A Q 7 6 4	◇ K 6	♣ A Q 8 6
c)	♠ 9 4	♡ A Q 6 2	◇ A K 4	♣ K 8 4 3
d)	♠ K 9 7 2	♡ A Q 7 6 4	◇ 8 3	♣ K 5
e)	♠ K J 5	♡ A Q 7 6 4	◇ 8 3 2	♣ A K

It only remains for you to agree with your partner the level to which you should play these takeout doubles. For simplicity, I suggest that a double of a supported suit at the two and three level should be for takeout.

Finally, how should we use the double of a forcing bid?

South	West	North	East
1♡	1♠	2♣	Double

If East had outstanding clubs he should lie in wait rather than prematurely warn North/South that they are heading for trouble. Therefore this double is also competitive. The message is that he has good diamonds and spade tolerance.

Quiz

1) What do you bid with these hands if you are North at *Game all* and West has overcalled South's 1♣ opening bid with 1♡?

a)	♠ K Q 6 3 2	♡ 9 5	◇ K 9 5	♣ 7 4 3
b)	♠ A 7 5 3	♡ 9 5	◇ K 9 5 2	♣ 7 4 3
c)	♠ 7 5 3	♡ K Q 10 8 2	◇ A J 6 2	♣ 7
d)	♠ 7 5 3	♡ 8 5 3 2	◇ K 9 5	♣ A J 4

2) What do you bid with these hands if you are North at *Love all* and West has overcalled South's 1♡ opening bid with 2♣?

a)	♠ Q 7 3 2	♡ 10 3 2	◇ A Q 4 3	♣ 8 4
b)	♠ Q 7 3 2	♡ 10	◇ Q 4 3 2	♣ A 4 3 2
c)	♠ Q 7 3 2	♡ 10	◇ A Q 4 3	♣ K 10 3 2

3) What do you call with these hands after the sequence below?

South	West	North	East
1◇	1♠	Double	No
?			

a)	♠ Q 7 3	♡ K Q 6 2	◇ A Q 8 7 2	♣ 8
b)	♠ A 7 3	♡ K Q 6 2	◇ A Q 8 7 2	♣ 8
c)	♠ 8 4 2	♡ K Q 6	◇ A Q 8 7 2	♣ Q 2

4) What do you call with these hands after the sequence below?

South	West	North	East
1♡	2♣	No	No
?			

a) ♠ Q 7 3   ♡ A Q 8 7 2   ◇ K Q 6 2   ♣ 2

b) ♠ Q 7 3   ♡ A Q 8 7 2   ◇ Q   ♣ A Q 6 2

c) ♠ 10 2   ♡ A K J 6 3 2   ◇ K Q 10 5 3   ♣ —

5) What do you call with these hands after the sequence below?

South	West	North	East
1♡	Double	2♡	?

a) ♠ J 8 3   ♡ 8 2   ◇ A 9 3 2   ♣ K 9 3 2

b) ♠ J 8 3 2   ♡ 8   ◇ A 9 3 2   ♣ K 9 3 2

c) ♠ Q 10 3 2   ♡ 8 2   ◇ A Q 3 2   ♣ K Q 3

d) ♠ 7 3   ♡ 9 8 3 2   ◇ A K Q 4   ♣ A J 3

e) ♠ 9 3   ♡ K Q J 10 8   ◇ Q 6 3   ♣ 6 4 3

6) What do you call with these hands after the sequence below?

South	West	North	East
1◇	1♠	2♣	2♠
?			

a) ♠ 8   ♡ K Q 7 2   ◇ A Q 8 7 4   ♣ K 9 2

b) ♠ 8   ♡ K Q 7   ◇ A Q 8 7 4   ♣ K 9 3 2

7) For each of these hands decide your call after the sequences below at *Love all*.

i)
South	West	North	East
1◇	1♡	No	?

ii)
South	West	North	East
1◇	1♡	2◇	?

iii)
South	West	North	East
1◇	1♡	3◇	?

a) ♠ 9 2   ♡ K 6 2   ◇ 10 6 3 2   ♣ K 8 3 2

b) ♠ 9   ♡ K 6 3 2   ◇ 10 6 3 2   ♣ K 8 3 2

c) ♠ 9   ♡ K 10 6 4 2   ◇ 7 3   ♣ K 6 4 3 2

d) ♠ K 9 2   ♡ Q 6 2   ◇ 6 3   ♣ A Q 8 3 2

e) ♠ A K 2   ♡ K 6 2   ◇ 6 3   ♣ A Q 8 3 2

Answers to quiz

1) a) 1♠, usually showing a five-card suit.
   b) Double. For takeout, promising 4 spades.
   c) Pass. You have a penalty double and expect South to re-open. If he doubles you are in business!
   d) 2♣. Don't double without 4 spades.

2) a) Double. An ideal Sputnik double as you are prepared for any response.
   b) Pass. You are not prepared for a 2♡ rebid.
   c) Double. This time you can remove a 2♡ rebid to 2NT. Pass is a reasonable alternative, intending to pass South's re-opening double.

3) a) 2♡. You would have raised a 1♡ response to 2♡.
   b) 3♡. You would have raised a 1♡ response to 3♡.
   c) 2◇. North will be prepared for this. An imaginative pairs alternative is 2♡. Most of the time this will be a 4-3 fit, but if North is not strong enough to bid a forcing 2♡ he might even have 5 hearts.

4) a) Double. For takeout, but you are conscious that North may be lurking, ready to pass. You must *not* pass as North may be very strong.
   b) Pass. Your clubs are so good that North cannot have a penalty double. Therefore he has a weak hand!
   c) 3◇. You are not interested in a penalty double because you have too great a disparity between your playing strength and defensive strength. Don't bid a meagre 2◇ because North will assume you are weak.

5) a) Double. Responsive and denying four spades. Let your partner choose the suit.
   b) 2♠. A responsive double would deny four spades. Even if this is a 4-3 fit you may score well by scrambling seven or eight tricks.
   c) 3♡. This time you intend to play in game so you are too strong for 2♠ or 3♠, neither of which is forcing. Raise 3♠ to 4♠, or pass a 3NT rebid. Note that an initial responsive double *denies* four spades.
   d) Double. Then follow up partner's choice of suit with 3♡,

hoping he can bid 3NT.

    e) Pass. A pity, but you don't have a penalty double available any more. If this is really your lucky day, West will re-open with another takeout double, which you will grate-fully pass!

6) a) Double. Competitive. You are prepared to play in hearts, diamonds, or clubs.

    b) 3♣. Show your support. Double may leave you in a 4-3 heart fit with a 5-4 club fit available.

7) a) i) 2♡. Mildly pre-emptive.

      ii) 2♡. Compete for the part score.

      iii) 3♡. Again, don't sell out too cheaply in the battle for the part scores. 3♡ will be right if *either* 3♢ *or* 3♡ makes.

    b) i) 3♡. Try to prevent your opponents from finding a spade fit.

      ii) 3♡. You won't buy this one with pathetic 2♡, indeed you will only make it easy for an opponent to try 2♠, and eventually outbid you in 3♠ over 3♡.

      iii) 3♡. Again don't sell out too quickly.

    c) i), ii) and iii) 4♡. Pre-empt to the limit!

    d) i) 2♢. An *Unassuming Cue Bid*, showing a game try in hearts.

      ii) 3♢. Again an Unassuming Cue Bid.

      iii) Double. This auction is too high for a cue bid to allow you to stop below game, therefore double fulfils that role.

    e) i) 2♢, followed by 4♡ next time. An immediate 4♡ would suggest a weak, shapely hand, like c).

      ii) 3♢, followed by 4♡.

      iii) Double followed by 4♡. The trouble with 4♢ is that it sounds like a slam try with first round diamond control.

9. Two-Suited Overcalls

You have already seen, in numerous different contexts, that to succeed at duplicate pairs you must be constantly and aggressively nosing your way into the auction. It is now worth standing back for a moment to examine how we deal with various types of hands once opponents open the bidding.

With a balanced hand you can overcall 1NT if you have 16-18 HCP (or 11-16 in the protective position, with the Crowhurst convention to enquire about range and four-card majors). If you have more than 18 HCP you start with a takeout double and then bid no trumps. With less that 16 HCP you generally pass, but you might upvalue a good 15 to 16, or make a takeout double if the vulnerability is right.

With a three-suited hand and shortage in opener's suit you make a takeout double and let partner decide the denomination.

With a one-suited hand you can make a simple one-level overcall with up to 15 HCP, or 17 at the two level. If you have a strong hand, with a good quality six-card suit that would have justified opening the bidding and jump rebidding your suit, you are worth a jump overcall. If your suit has only five cards you must double first and then bid your suit at the lowest legal level. Note that in the sequence below, West is showing a strong one suited hand, not a two-suiter! The commonly held view that 'he doesn't like clubs so he has hearts and spades' has no foundation.

South	West	North	East
1◇	Dbl	No	2♣
No	2♡		

So how do we show two-suiters? Suppose your right-hand opponent opens 1♣ at *Love all* and you hold these hands:

a) ♠ K J 10 7 4   ♡ Q J 8 7 5   ◇ 9 6   ♣ 3
b) ♠ K Q 10 7 4   ♡ A Q J 9 8   ◇ 9 6   ♣ 3
c) ♠ A K 10 7 4   ♡ A Q J 9 8   ◇ A 6   ♣ 3

With a) there is some risk in entering the bidding at all, but if you can show both suits quickly the prospect of finding a fit increases, and the risk correspondingly diminishes. That will be impossible unless you can show both suits in one bid, because you are far too weak to enter the auction twice freely. The key is to develop a system of two-suited overcalls. Before describing the details you must understand the principles of valuation of a two-suiter.

There are three categories:

   i) Weak. 6-10 HCP; for example, hand a).
  ii) Intermediate. 11-15 HCP. Hand b).
 iii) Strong. 16+ HCP. Hand c).

THE MICHAELS CUE BID

If an opponent opens with a minor suit an immediate cue bid in his suit shows a major two-suiter. This uses up a whole round of bidding, and if you can have a), b) or c) partner will always be unsure of how high to go. The answer is to only use this bid for Weak or Strong hands. (If you hold an intermediate hand like b), start with a simple overcall (1♠) and bid your heart suit on the next round, providing the bidding comes back to you at a reasonable level.) For his initial response partner will assume you have the weak type.

	South	West	North	East
	1◇	2◇	No	?

d)	♠ Q 8 6	♡ K 7 5 4	◇ 9 5 3 2	♣ 10 4
e)	♠ Q 8 5	♡ Q 9 5 4 2	◇ 9 6 4 3 2	♣ −
f)	♠ Q J 5	♡ Q 7 6 3	◇ A K 9	♣ A 4 2

With d) East bids a quiet 2♡. If West has the weak type that is quite high enough, but if West subsequently shows a strong hand by raising to 3♡ East will gladly bid game, which will be laydown if West has c).

With e) and f) East wants to bid game, but for very different reasons. With e) he wants to pre-empt if West is weak, and expects to succeed if West is strong. He shows this by an immediate jump to 4♡. With f) he expects to succeed if West is weak, doesn't fear opponents interfering, and has every reason to seek a slam if West is strong. He starts with a return cue bid of 3◇ and bids 4♡ next time if West can do no more than show the weak type with a simple rebid. The principle is similar to making a delayed game raise in an uncontested auction.

If opponents open a major suit an immediate cue bid shows the other major suit and an unspecified minor, again either weak or strong. Partner can ask which minor with the artificial 2NT response, and if the overcalling cue bidder has the strong type he must jump in his minor suit.

In general all these two-suited bids should show at least 5-5 shape, but it may be tactically opportune to overcall a minor suit with a Michaels Cue Bid at green vulnerability if you are weak and your major suits have only 5-4 shape.

THE UNUSUAL NO TRUMP

An immediate 2NT overcall over an opponent's suit opening bid shows a two-suited hand with the two lowest of the remaining three suits. Thus 2NT over 1♡ or 1♠ shows the minor suits, while over 1♣ or 1♢ it shows hearts and the other minor. No doubt you have played this convention for years, but has it ever occurred to you to only use it for weak or strong hands? The reasoning is the same as with Michaels Cue Bids.

THE ASTRO DEFENCE TO 1NT

When recommending the weak no trump in chapter 6 I praised its pre-emptive effectiveness, and described how you often score well in 1NT even if you fail to make the contract. The need to harass opponents out of 1NT is therefore even more pressing than if they open with a suit bid. Paradoxically, it is not only harder (because one-level overcalls are not available and you need far more to double), but also more dangerous because if you do get it wrong your opponents are well placed to judge a penalty double. You want to compete with a hand like b) on p. 67 but only if you can show both of your suits. Strong hands don't enter the equation this time because you either make a penalty double or the game-forcing 2NT overcall, so the practical strength of suit overcalls is intermediate, or weak if the vulnerability is right. Since the purpose of these two-suited overcalls is mainly competitive rather than constructive, 5-4 shape is acceptable.

The following defence to 1NT is called *Astro*:

Double for penalties with 16+ points.
2♣ shows hearts and a minor suit. At least 5-4 shape.
2♢ shows spades and another suit. Again at least 5-4 shape.
2♡ and 2♠ are natural overcalls with a good six-card suit.

2NT shows a strong two-suited hand, game-forcing with at least 5-5 shape. The trouble with doubling on very shapely hands is that declarer can often run too many quick tricks in your short suits. After a 2NT overcall partner tries to keep the bidding low to enable you to show your suits cheaply and should, for example, prefer to bid 3♣ on a three-card suit rather than consume bidding space.

i)	South	West	North	East	ii)	South	West	North	East
	1NT	2♣	No	?		1NT	2♢	No	?

After each of these sequences East knows one of West's suits, called the *Anchor Suit* (hearts in auction i) and spades in auction ii)). He can sign off in this suit at the two level or jump constructively to a higher level. Alternatively he can enquire about the second suit with 2NT. A third option, particularly useful if he is weak and not happy with the anchor suit, is to bid the suit in between the conventional overcall and the anchor suit. He would bid 2♢ in auction i) with:

♠ 9 6 3   ♡ 10 7   ♢ 9 7 3   ♣ A Q 6 4 2

This instructs West to pass if he has five diamonds, or otherwise bid his cheapest five-card suit. If West rebids 2♡ East must pass, but at least that will not be a 4-2 fit!

DEFENDING AGAINST STRONG 1♣ SYSTEMS

All the strong club systems you are likely to meet have the common feature of an opening 1♣ showing a strong hand, and a 1♢ response being the weakness reply. Your method of defence should be determined by the nature of these bids.

Firstly, because 1♣ is strong, your main priority is to create problems for your opponents rather than to bid constructively to game.

Secondly, because 1♣ is forcing (as is the 1♢ reply) you will get a second chance if you pass on the first round. Indeed, if you want to bid constructively you will probably find it far easier to do so on the second round of bidding, by which time you will usually have a natural bid to defend against. By this time you can use your normal systemic methods.

Therefore you pass on the first round with any hand with 15 or more HCP.

South	West	North	East
1♣	No	1◇	No
1♡	?		

a)	♠ A Q 7 5	♡ 8	◇ A K 8 2	♣ K J 7 3
b)	♠ A Q 9 8 4	♡ 8 4	◇ A K 8	♣ K 9 7
c)	♠ A Q J	♡ A Q 8	◇ K Q 7	♣ J 8 7 3
d)	♠ A Q 8 6 5	♡ 9	◇ A K J 6 4	♣ K 2

Having passed on the first round West makes a takeout double with a), overcalls 1♠ with b) and 1NT with c), and ventures a Michaels Cue Bid of 2♡ with d).

You should only bid on the first round if you are intermediate or weak, aiming to indicate a lead, pave the way for a profitable sacrifice, or just make it hard for your opponents to compare notes. Over a strong 1♣ opening, or a 1♣ opening and a negative 1◇ response, I recommend the following system of weak jump overcalls and two-suited overcalls, called *Truscott*.

Jump overcalls are natural, one-suited, and weak. They show a suit of reasonable quality, rather like a weak two-opening. They suggest a six-card suit, but at Green vulnerability a five-card suit with good intermediate cards will suffice. Once again in duplicate pairs, the objective is to be as obstructive as you dare!

A suit overcall without a jump shows the suit bid and the next higher one, with at least 5-4 shape.

Double shows the suit doubled and the non-touching one.

1NT shows the other two non-touching suits.

i) South	West	ii) South	West	iii) South	West
1♣	1♠	1♣	Double	1♣	1NT

iv) South	West	North	East	v) South	West	North	East
1♣	No	1◇	Double	1♣	No	1◇	1NT

In auction i) West has spades and clubs. In ii) he has clubs and hearts. In iii) he has diamonds and spades. In iv) East has

diamonds and spades while in v) he has hearts and clubs. In each
case the overcaller's partner, having given due consideration to
the vulnerability, should know what to do!

Quiz
1) For each of these hands what do you bid after the auctions
   below? If appropriate, decide also on your plan for the next
   round of bidding.

	Love all		*North/South Game*		*East/West Game*	
i)	South	West	ii) South	West	iii) South	West
	1◇	?	1NT	?	1♣ *	?

	North/South Game			*North/South Game*		
iv)	South	West	v) South	West	North	East
	1♣ *	?	1♣ *	No	1◇ $	?

* 1♣ is conventional, forcing, and showing at least 16 HCP.
\$ 1◇ is conventional, forcing, and showing 0-7 HCP.

a) ♠ Q J 10 6 3   ♡ K J 10 3 2   ◇ J 7   ♣ 7
b) ♠ A K J 6 3   ♡ K J 10 3 2   ◇ 10 7   ♣ 7
c) ♠ A K J 6 3   ♡ A K 10 3 2   ◇ A 7   ♣ 7
d) ♠ A K J 9 6 5   ♡ A K J 10 4   ◇ 8   ♣ 7
e) ♠ 10 7   ♡ K J 10 3 2   ◇ 8   ♣ Q J 10 6 3
f) ♠ A K J 6 3   ♡ K 7   ◇ 8   ♣ A K 10 6 3

2) What do you bid with these hands at *Love all*?

South	West	North	East
1♡	2♡	No	?

a) ♠ K 9 4 2   ♡ 9 4 2   ◇ A 9 3 2   ♣ 8 4
b) ♠ K 9 4 3 2 ♡ 9 4 2   ◇ A 9 3 2   ♣ 8
c) ♠ K J 4 2   ♡ A 4 2   ◇ A K 3 2   ♣ Q 4

3) Playing Astro, what do you bid with these hands after this
   sequence at *Love all*?

South	West	North	East
1NT	2◇	No	?

a) ♠ K J 8   ♡ 9 3   ◇ 8 3   ♣ K Q 8 7 3 2
b) ♠ K J 8   ♡ 9 4 3   ◇ 10 7 2   ♣ K Q 8 7
c) ♠ 6   ♡ A J 5 2 ◇ K Q J 10   ♣ A 10 9 8
d) ♠ K J 6 2 ♡ 9 3   ◇ K 9 8 3 2 ♣ A 7

4) Plan your strategy with these hands at *Green* vulnerability if your right-hand opponent opens a strong 1♣?

a) ♠ A Q J 7 3 2   ♡ 7 3 2   ◇ 9 3   ♣ 10 2
b) ♠ A J 7 3 2   ♡ 3 2   ◇ K 9 3   ♣ A 10 2
c) ♠ A J 10 8   ♡ 3 2   ◇ 9 2   ♣ Q J 10 5 2
d) ♠ A Q J 7 3 2   ♡ A 3 2   ◇ A Q   ♣ 10 2
e) ♠ K J 7 3   ♡ 9   ◇ A K 8 3 ♣ A K J 10

5) At *Green* vulnerability South opens a strong 1♣, West (your partner) overcalls 1NT, and North passes. What do you bid with these hands?

a) ♠ K J 6 3 2   ♡ 8   ◇ J 10 7 5 2   ♣ 8 3
b) ♠ 8   ♡ K J 6 3 2   ◇ 8 3   ♣ J 10 7 5 2
c) ♠ K 7 5 2   ♡ 9 5 2   ◇ J 8   ♣ 8 4 3 2

Answers to quiz

1) a)   i) 2◇. A Michaels Cue Bid showing the major suits.
        ii) 2◇. Astro showing spades and another suit.
        iii) Pass. Too dangerous to bid at *Red* vulnerability.
        iv) 1♡. Truscott showing hearts and spades.
        v) 1♡. Truscott, as in iv).

   b)   i) 1♠. This is an *intermediate* strength hand and is there-fore unsuitable for a Michaels Cue Bid. As long as you can do so at a reasonable level, bid hearts next time.
        ii) 2◇. Astro showing spades and another suit.
        iii) 1♡. This time you are strong enough to compete, even at *Red* vulnerability.
        iv) 1♡. As hand a).
        v) 1♡. Truscott again.

   c)   i) 2◇. The strong variety of Michaels Cue Bid. Raise whichever suit East chooses to the three level.
        ii) Double. For penalties. You are too strong for 2◇.
        iii), and iv) Pass. You are *too strong* to compete on the first round after a strong club opening bid. North will probably respond 1◇ and you can show your assets on the next round with an Astro 2◇ over 1NT, or a Michaels Cue Bid over a minor suit rebid. If South rebids a major you must be content with a simple overcall of the other major.
        v) Again you are too strong to bid on the first round. If South makes a natural rebid and North passes your action

will be similar to iii) and iv) above. However, if South and North both bid there will be times when you will have to also pass next time.

d) i) Start with 2♢, then raise 2♠ to 4♠, or jump to 3♠ over 2♡, forcing and showing at least 6-5 shape.

ii) 2NT. Insist on game in one of your suits. Doubling 1NT would run the risk of opener making it with minor suit tricks.

iii), iv) and v) Pass. On the second round your bidding will be similar to c), but this time you will not stop short of game.

e) i) 2NT, showing the lower two of the three unbid suits. Or pass if you feel cautious!

ii) 2♣. Astro, showing hearts and a minor suit.

iii) Pass. Take heed of the vulnerability!

iv) Double. Truscott showing hearts and clubs.

v) 1NT. Truscott, again!

f) i) Double. You don't have a two-suited overcall available and you are too strong for 1♠. Rebid 1♠ if partner responds 1♡, but unfortunately that shows a strong, one-suited spade hand, not a two-suiter.

ii) Double. For penalties.

iii), iv) and v) Pass. Try an Astro 2♢ after a natural 1NT by South, a Michaels 2♡ over 1♡, or a minimum spade overcall otherwise.

2) a) 2♠. If West is weak that is high enough, while if he is strong he will bid on.

b) 4♠. Pre-emptive.

c) 3♡. Then 4♠ next time. This tells your partner your game bid is based on high cards, not just shape.

3) a) 2♠. This may be a 4-3 fit, but a 5-2 fit at the three level is hardly more attractive.

b) 2♡. If West has 5 hearts he will pass, otherwise he will bid his cheapest five-card suit. You are bound to find a 5-3 fit at worst.

c) 2NT. If his second suit is hearts play in 4♡, otherwise in 3NT.

d) 3♠. Invitational.

4) a) 2♠. A weak jump overcall.
   b) Pass. Unfortunately you will not find it easy to enter this auction as a second round bid will show strength!
   c) 1♠. Weak, showing the black suits.
   d) Pass. Then spades next time.
   e) Pass. Probably North will respond 1◇. Your second round action will then depend on South's rebid. Double 1♡ for takeout, or 1NT for penalties. Overcall 1♠ with 1NT, but perhaps it is wise to pass 2♣ or 2◇.

5) Partner has a weak or intermediate hand with spades and diamonds. If you have anything like a fit you must pre-empt as high as you dare before they get their act together.
   a) 4♠. An advance sacrifice! You have a fit in two suits, and so have your opponents! Your advantage is that they don't know it.
   b) Pass. Horrible!
   c) 3♠. They must have a laydown vulnerable game.

10. Opponents Interfere over Partner's 1NT

Lebensohl

Having learned how to interfere with opponent's 1NT contract in chapter 9 you now need a system of dealing with interference to your 1NT. Suppose your right-hand opponent overcalls your partner's 1NT with 2♡. If you want to bid to game the overcall has created two new problems for you. Firstly, you no longer have the Stayman 2♣ bid available to search for a 4-4 spade fit. Secondly, you might want reassurance that there is adequate cover in their suit before settling for no trumps. The excellent *Lebensohl* convention goes a long way to solving these problems.

i) 2NT by responder requires opener to rebid 3♣. The sequence can now be used for two purposes.

a) With a weak hand responder can use it for signing off at the three level. If his suit is clubs he will pass the 3♣ relay; if he has diamonds he will convert to 3◇.

b) Responder can use it to show a balanced, or semi-balanced hand with game values, but *no guard in their suit*. If he follows up with a cue bid of 3♡ he is showing a four-card major (obviously spades in this case) or if he follows up with 3NT he is denying a spade suit. If no spade suit fit exists and the hearts are unguarded opener will retreat to 4♣ or 4◇.

ii) An immediate cue bid by responder (in this case 3♡) shows a heart guard and four spades. Opener will find it easy to pick the contract.

iii) An immediate 3NT by responder shows a heart guard and denies four spades. 3NT will plainly be the final contract.

iv) A new suit at the three level by responder is natural and game-forcing, showing a five-card suit (or perhaps six if the suit is a minor.)

The following table summarises responder's policy with a *balanced hand* if opener's 1NT is overcalled with 2♡.

	4 spades	Less than 4 spades
Heart guard	Responder bids an immediate 3♡	Responder bids an immediate 3NT
No heart guard	Responder bids 2NT, then 3♡ over 3♣	Responder bids 2NT, then 3NT over 3♣

If responder does not have game values he can compete for the part-score, or invite game. A suit at the two level (2♠) is a sign-off, and double is used in a Sputnik context, showing a balanced or semi-balanced hand worth a game try. Opener is *not* expected to re-open if responder passes! Responder's ability to make a penalty double is obviously lost, but there is some compensation in that if opener has particularly good hearts he can sometimes make a penalty pass. Playing pairs he should be on the lookout for this opportunity if opponents are vulnerable!

What if your partner opens 1NT and your right-hand opponent makes a conventional overcall? Most conventional overcalls have a known suit (called the *Anchor* suit). In the example below East/West are playing Astro, so 2♣ shows hearts and a minor suit.

South	West	North	East
1NT	2♣	?	

If you are strong you should react as though the overcall was 2♡. Admittedly, that might get you to 3NT with no guard in West's second suit, but as you have no way of discovering his second suit there is no point in worrying about it!

If you are not strong enough to demand game you can bid the known anchor suit at the two level for takeout (2♡), so double is available to suggest that it might be desirable to make a penalty double of their final resting place.

a) ♠ Q J 7 4   ♡ K 8   ◇ A Q J 4   ♣ 9 5 2
b) ♠ Q J 7 4   ♡ 9 8   ◇ A Q J 4   ♣ K 5 2
c) ♠ Q J 8 5   ♡ 7   ◇ A Q 8 5   ♣ Q 8 5 2
d) ♠ Q 7 2   ♡ A J 9 3   ◇ K J 7 2   ♣ 9 3

With a) bid 3♡, showing a heart guard and four spades. With b) bid 2NT and continue with 3♡ after 3♣. If South converts to 4♣ you must pass.
With c) bid 2♡, for takeout.
With d) double. You will be delighted to double 2♡ or 2◇, and won't object if partner wants to double a club contract.

WRIGGLING FROM 1NT DOUBLED

If you play the weak no trump you must expect to suffer the occasional large penalty as an occupational hazard! However, if you play a 'Wriggle' it is surprising the number of times opponents don't feel confident enough to double your escape suit, even if you have staggered into a 4-3 fit! Here is a simple wriggle system. If West doubles South's 1NT:

i) North can make a weakness takeout into a five-card suit by redoubling. South is compelled to rebid 2♣ and North will pass if he has five clubs, or sign off in his suit.

ii) If North has no five-card suit, but at least two four-card suits he bids the *lower ranking* of his suits. Thus:

2♣ shows clubs and another suit.

2♦ shows diamonds and a major suit.

2♡ shows hearts and spades.

With three or more in the suit bid South passes, even if he is doubled. Alternatively, if he has only a doubleton he bids the lowest suit he can tolerate (i.e., with at least three cards). Of course this can sometimes result in playing in a 4-3 fit when a 4-4 fit is available, but in practice opponents find it extraordinarily difficult to double because they have never discussed whether double is for penalties or takeout! If they end up subsiding into their own contract, your gamble has paid off.

Quiz

1) Plan your strategy as North for the hands below after this sequence at RED vulnerability.

South	West	North
1NT	2♦ *	?

*2♦ shows spades and another suit.

a)	♠ 8 4	♡ K J 7 4	♦ K 8 5	♣ A K 6 3
b)	♠ K 4	♡ A J 8 4	♦ K 8 5	♣ A 6 3 2
c)	♠ 8 4 2	♡ K J 7	♦ K 8 5	♣ A K 6 3
d)	♠ K 4 2	♡ K J 2	♦ K 8 5	♣ A 8 6 3
e)	♠ K Q 10 5	♡ 9 6	♦ Q 8 5	♣ A 8 6 3
f)	♠ 9 6	♡ K Q 10 5	♦ Q 8 5	♣ A 8 6 3
g)	♠ 9 5	♡ A 8 2	♦ 9 6	♣ A K J 7 4 2
h)	♠ 9 5	♡ A 8 2	♦ 9 6	♣ K J 10 7 4 2
i)	♠ 9 5	♡ K J 10 7 4 2	♦ 9 6	♣ A 8 2

2) What is your next bid with the hands below after each of these sequences?

i)	South	West	North	East	ii)	South	West	North	East
	1NT	2♡	3♡	No		1NT	2♣ *	2NT	No
	?					3♣	No	3♡	No
						?			

iii)	South	West	North	East	iv)	South	West	North	East
	1NT	2♡	3NT	No		1NT	2♣ *	2NT	No
	?					3♣	No	3NT	No
						?			

*2♣ shows hearts and a minor suit.

a) ♠ K Q 7 2   ♡ 9 5 2   ◇ A J 4   ♣ K 8 3
b) ♠ K Q 7 2   ♡ K 5 2   ◇ A J 4   ♣ 10 8 3
c) ♠ K Q 7   ♡ K 5 2   ◇ A J 4   ♣ 10 8 3 2
d) ♠ K Q 7   ♡ 9 5 2   ◇ A J 4   ♣ K 8 3 2

3) Plan your strategy as North at *Game all* with these hands if West doubles South's 1NT.

a) ♠ 9 2   ♡ Q 10 7 4 3   ◇ 9 6 3   ♣ 10 6 2
b) ♠ J 10 5 2   ♡ 9 2   ◇ J 9 6 4   ♣ 9 5 3

Answers to quiz

1) a) Bid 2NT, denying a spade guard, and then 3♠ over the compulsory 3♣, showing 4 hearts.
   b) Bid 3♠, showing a spade guard and 4 hearts.
   c) Bid 2NT, and follow it up with 3NT to deny 4 hearts.
   d) Bid 3NT, showing a spade guard and denying 4 hearts.
   e) Double. Suggesting a desire to double spades.
   f) 2♠. Bid the anchor suit for takeout.
   g) 3♣. Forcing. If opener rebids 3NT you should pass.
   h) 2NT, and pass the forced 3♣ rebid.
   i) 2♡. A sign-off.

2) a) i) and ii) 3♠. Forcing. North has 4 spades.
        iii) Pass. 3NT denies 4 spades but shows a heart guard.
        iv) 4♠. With neither of you having a heart guard 3NT cannot be right, and provided South has three-card support this might work well!
   b) i) and ii) 3♠, as with a).
        iii) Pass. Obvious.
        iv) Pass. North hasn't got a heart guard, but this time you have!
   c) You have a heart guard but not 4 spades. In each case 3NT is the correct contract, so either bid it or pass North's 3NT.
   d) i) 3NT. North has a heart guard.
       ii) 3♠, on a 4-3 fit. Can you think of a better idea?

iii) Pass. Again North has a heart guard.

iv) 4♣. 3NT would be hopeless.

3) a) Redouble, and bid 2♡ over South's compulsory 2♣.

    b) Bid 2◇, the lower of your four-card suits. If South rebids 2♡ try 2♠!

11. The Multi-Coloured 2◇ Bid

Whether you love or hate the Multi, you cannot ignore it if you play duplicate pairs! It is the most common of an increasing number of conventions that use a single bid to describe a wide variety of hands. The 2◇ opening bid is used to cover three (or more) different hand types.

    i) A weak 2♠ opening bid. i.e. 6-10 HCP and six spades.

    ii) A weak 2♡ opening bid. i.e. 6-10 HCP and six hearts.

    iii) One, or more, type(s) of strong hand(s).

If you play the Multi with straight Acol you have to relinquish a strong Acol 2◇ opening bid (instead, opening such hands at the one level or with 2♣, just as you do with a club suit). In return you get a gadget that is highly pre-emptive, and most difficult to defend against. The secret of its effectiveness is that if your side has the balance of power your partner can easily find out your suit, and values, and almost anything else he wants to know. But if your opponents want to enter the auction they must often do so without knowing your suit. This poses plenty of problems for them, for instance:

    i) They have no cue bid available.

    ii) It is not easy to make a penalty or takeout double unless you know which suit you are penalising, or competing against.

    iii) It is difficult to bid no trumps without knowing which suit you are supposed to be guarding.

There are defences to the Multi available, and later in this chapter I outline one, but they are all rather clumsy and you can have a field-day watching unprepared opponents floundering in confusion.

If you open 2◇ responder assumes you have a weak two bid. Often he is prepared to play in your suit. In that case if the next hand passes he responds as follows:

2♡ instructs you to pass if you have a weak 2♡ opening, or convert to 2♠ if you have a weak 2♠ bid. He might have a), with no ambitions beyond a part score whatever your suit, or b) when he will delighted to jump to 4♠ if you rebid 2♠.

2♠ instructs you to pass if you have spades, or convert to 3♡ with hearts. He has better hearts than spades—hand c).

3♡ is mildly pre-emptive, and asks you to pass or correct to 3♠. He might have d).

4♡ asks you to pass, or bid 4♠. His purpose might be pre-emptive, e), or constructive, f). You don't know and, more significantly, neither do your opponents!

a)	♠ 7 4	♡ 9 5	◇ K Q 6 3	♣ A 7 5 3 2
b)	♠ K Q 5 2	♡ 6	◇ A Q 8 6 3	♣ K 8 2
c)	♠ 6	♡ K Q 5 2	◇ A Q 8 6 3	♣ K 8 2
d)	♠ K 8 6	♡ K 8 7 2	◇ 10 9 7 5	♣ 10 3
e)	♠ K J 8 4	♡ K 8 5 2	◇ 9 7 5 3 2	♣ —
f)	♠ K 8	♡ A J 7	◇ K Q 7 4	♣ A Q 7 3

If responder changes suit with a forcing 3♣, 3◇ or 3♠, opener will normally rebid his suit. (Remember, responder doesn't know it!)

Alternatively, if responder wants more detailed information about opener's assets and is prepared to advance to the three level whatever his suit and values, he can use the conventional 2NT response which is used as an asking bid. Opener must now classify his weak two bid as minimum or maximum; maximum being defined as having 8½-10 points, or two of the top three honours, or both. He then rebids as follows:

> 3♣ = Maximum weak 2♡ bid.
> 3◇ = Maximum weak 2♠ bid.
> 3♡ = Minimum weak 2♡ bid.
> 3♠ = Minimum weak 2♠ bid.

After 3♣ or 3◇ responder can bid the other major suit (natural and forcing), declare the final contract, or unambiguously agree opener's suit and enquire further by bidding the suit in between the conventional rebid and the trump suit. For example:

West	East	
2◇	2NT (1)	(1) Enquiry bids.
3♣ (2)	3◇ (1)	(2) Maximum weak 2♡ opening bid.
? (3)		(3) 3♡ = 6-8 HCP. Two of the top three heart honours.

$3♠$ = 8½-10 HCP. Not two top hearts.

3NT = 8½-10 HCP *and* two top hearts.

The strong variety of Multi opening

It makes sense to pick the type of strong hand that causes you most problems, and incorporate it into the Multi. Strong 4-4-4-1 shape hands are difficult to handle at Acol, so why not open them 2◇? Apart from solving some hands in the 21-23 HCP range which don't have a good enough suit for an Acol two-bid, are not strong enough for an Acol 2♣, but are too strong for a one-level opening, a consequential gain is that if you open an Acol 2♣ and rebid a suit, your suit has at least five cards.

Of course responder will initially assume you have a weak two bid, but you can open his eyes by rebidding the bid below the singleton.

i) West	East	ii) West	East	iii) West	East	iv) West	East
2◇	2♡	2◇	2♠	2◇	2♠	2◇	2♠
2NT		3◇		3♠		3◇	3♡
						?	

Thus in i) West has a singleton club and in ii) a singleton heart. The exception is iii). 3♠ shows a singleton *spade* because 3♡ is needed for a weak 2♡ opening.

Responder can, and should, continue by asking for details of opener's point count by bidding the singleton suit. In iv) West will continue with 3♠ (the lowest legal bid) to show 21-22 HCP, 3NT (the second cheapest bid) to show 23-24 HCP, 4♣ to show 25-26 HCP etc.

Defending against the Multi

Don't expect miracles here! The Multi is meant to make life awkward, and by and large it does a pretty good job!

After any opponent's opening bid the immediate and protective hands have different roles. This is even more true after a Multi 2◇ because the next hand *knows* it will get another chance. On the other hand after the sequence: 2◇ No 2♡ opener can pass, so you may never get another bite at the cherry.

Firstly examine the decision you face as West if South opens 2◇. You must choose one of the following ideas.
i) Pass on the first round if you have a strong hand, waiting until you know their suit. Bid on the first round if you have a weak, shapely hand when you want to make a competitive noise before the bidding gets too high.
Alternatively:
ii) Bid on the first round if you are strong, before your opponents have a chance to pre-empt. Pass with a weaker hand and protect later if appropriate.

The following defence is based on the principles of ii).
Immediately after a Multi 2◇ opening bid you require 16 points (or equivalent playing strength) to compete.

a)	♠ A J 10 8 2	♡ 9 7	◇ K Q 8	♣ A K 8
b)	♠ A J 10 8 2	♡ 9 7	◇ K J 8	♣ A 8 7
c)	♠ A Q 5	♡ Q 10 4	◇ K Q 9	♣ A J 8 7
d)	♠ A Q 6 4	♡ 9	◇ K Q 8 6	♣ A K 9 2
e)	♠ A K 6	♡ K Q 8 5	◇ Q 9 8	♣ A K 10
f)	♠ A K J 8 7	♡ 10 6	◇ A K J	♣ A Q 4

Overcall 2♠ with a) (16-20 points), but pass with b) and await developments. If responder's 2♡ is followed by two passes you can protect with 2♠ which is now limited to 15 points because of your pass on the first round.

Overcall 2NT with c), showing 16-19 HCP and a guard in both majors. Partner's responses mean the same as they would do over a 2NT opening bid, but he will allow for the fact that your 2NT overcall is weaker than a 2NT opening bid.

Other strong hands, like d), e), and f), must be introduced with a double, which overloads it dangerously. Therefore to ensure that you have time to compare notes if you have combined game values, partner needs to have one conventional 'negative' response available showing 0-7 points. The negative response is the lowest legal call that allows the doubler another chance, i.e., 2♡ in sequence i) and pass in sequence ii). Other responses are game-forcing.

i)   South   West   North East   ii)   South   West   North East
    2◇   Double No   ?   2◇   Double 2♡   ?

iii) South   West North East   iv) South   West North East
    2◇   No   2♡   ?   2◇   No   2♠   ?

Finally, what principles should guide East if West passes and North bids 2♡? After iii) East knows that he will not get another bid *if South's suit is hearts*. Therefore he imagines the auction has gone 2♡ (weak) No No ? With hand g) he doubles for takeout (no negative response needed this time), with h) he bids 2NT, showing 17-20 HCP and a heart guard, and with j) he passes. If the auction proceeds with South rebidding 2♠ he now *knows* he is defending against a weak 2♠ opening so he can double protectively for takeout.

    Alternatively, after sequence iv) East passes with g), bids 2NT with h) and doubles with j) as this time he will not get another chance if South's suit is spades. Obviously he must be a little more cautious after this sequence because of the implication that North has respectable hearts.

g) ♠ K Q 6 4   ♡ 8   ◇ A Q 7 3   ♣ K 8 4 2
h) ♠ K J 6 4   ♡ A J 6   ◇ A Q 7 3   ♣ K 2
j)   ♠ 8   ♡ K Q 6 4 ◇ A Q 7 3   ♣ K 8 4 2

Quiz

1) What do you respond to your partner's Multi 2◇ opening at *Love all* with these hands?

a) ♠ A J 7   ♡ 8   ◇ K J 10 2   ♣ A 8 4 3 2
b) ♠ 8   ♡ A J 7   ◇ K J 10 2   ♣ A 8 4 3 2
c) ♠ A Q 8 5 ♡ J 9 5 3 ◇ K 4   ♣ A K 2
d) ♠ J 5   ♡ Q 6   ◇ A K 7 3   ♣ A K J 3 2
e) ♠ 7   ♡ K 10   ◇ A K Q 7 6 4 2 ♣ K 7 2
f) ♠ K J 2   ♡ 9 4   ◇ A Q 8 4   ♣ K Q 7 3

2) Having opened a Multi 2◇ with these hands, what is your rebid if partner responds 2NT?

a) ♠ A J 10 7 6 3   ♡ 9 6   ◇ Q 3 2   ♣ 8 3
b) ♠ A J 10 7 6 3   ♡ 9 6   ◇ K J 2   ♣ 8 3
c) ♠ A Q J 10 6 3   ♡ 9 6   ◇ 9 3 2   ♣ 8 3
d) ♠ A Q J 10 6 3   ♡ 9 6   ◇ Q 3 2   ♣ 8 3

3) With hands b), c), and d) of question 2), state your third bid if responder continues with the cheapest legal bid after your rebid?

4) Having opened a Multi 2◇ with these hands, what is your rebid if partner responds 2♡? What is your third bid if he continues with the cheapest legal bid?

a) ♠ K Q 7 4   ♡ A Q J 5   ◇ A K Q 6   ♣ 5
b) ♠ K Q 7 4   ♡ A   ◇ A Q J 5   ♣ A K Q 6

5) With these hands what is your call at *Love all*:
   i) As West if South opens 2◇?
   ii) As East if South opens 2◇ and North responds 2♡?

a) ♠ K J 6   ♡ 7   ◇ A Q 6 4 2   ♣ K Q 7 3
b) ♠ A K 6   ♡ 7   ◇ A Q 6 4 2   ♣ K Q 7 3
c) ♠ K Q 10 5 3 ♡ 9 5   ◇ A Q 8   ♣ Q 10 2

Answers to quiz

1) a) 2♡. Quite high enough if partner has a weak 2♡ opening. If he rebids 2♠ you will be delighted to jump to 4♠. You will score well on this hand by avoiding trouble as many pairs will be unable to stop in time!
   b) 2♠. To play opposite a weak 2♠ opening. Raise a 3♡ rebid to 4♡.
   c) 4♡. To play in 4♡ or 4♠, depending on opener's suit.
   d) 4♡. As above. A 6-2 fit will provide a perfectly adequate trump suit.
   e) 3◇. Opener will rebid his suit. Raise 3♡ to 4♡, or play in 3NT if he has spades.
   f) 2NT. If he rebids 3◇ or 3♠ you should take advantage of the excellent nine-card fit to raise to game. If he shows a featureless weak 2♡ bid with 3♡, pass. If he rebids 3♣

ask again with 3♦, prepared to pass 3♡ (minimum points, maximum suit quality) and chance 4♡ over 3♠ (maximum points, minimum suit quality).

2) a) 3♠. Spade suit, minimum points, minimum suit.
   b), c) and d) 3♦. Spade suit. Either maximum points, or two of the top three trumps, or both.

3) b) Rebid 3NT over 3♡. Maximum points, not two top trumps.
   c) Rebid 3♠ over 3♡. Minimum points, two top trumps.
   d) Rebid 4♣ over 3♡. Maximum points, two top trumps.

4) a) Rebid 2NT, showing a singleton club. Continue with 3♦ over 3♣ showing 21-22 HCP.
   b) Rebid 3♦, showing a singleton heart. Continue with 4♣ over 3♡ showing 25-26 HCP.

5) a) i) Pass. You are too weak to bid.
      ii) Double. A takeout double of a 2♡ opening.
   b) i) Double. You have a strong hand and no other bid.
      ii) Double, as with a).
   c) i) Pass. Like with a). Protect with 2♠ if appropriate.
      ii) 2♠. This could be your last chance!

Part 3   Declarer Play

12. Declarer Play When the Hand is Progressing Normally

As declarer at rubber bridge you have a clear aim, to fulfil your contract. However, playing duplicate pairs fulfilling your contract without overtricks may give you a bottom. Conversely, sometimes escaping for one off may be worth a top, indeed even −500 may be a triumph if your opponents can make a vulnerable game!

Often you can search for valuable overtricks with little risk to your contract, but sometimes you may have to decide whether to settle for safely fulfilling your contract, or taking risks to improve your score. The secret of success is learning to anticipate how many tricks you need for a good score. The key is to ask whether events at your table so far have been either:

a) Normal, when you must judge your actions strictly on their merits.

b) Particularly favourable to you, in which case you may not need overtricks for a good score. Perhaps you have bid to an excellent contract that most pairs are likely to miss, or you have been given a cheap trick on the opening lead.

c) Unfavourable, meaning that unless you can achieve something over and above the rest of the field from now on you are heading for a bad score. Perhaps you are in a slightly inferior contract, or the defenders have struck gold with an opening lead that you can tell was far from obvious. If you have good reason to believe that other pairs will declare the same contract from the opposite hand (perhaps because you have used a transfer bid sequence and you know most other pairs don't play transfers), it is often the case that the opening lead will not be standard.

In this chapter we examine decisions in which you have no particular reason to believe that what has already occurred differs from other tables.

West	East	West	East
♠ A Q 5	♠ K 3 2	1NT	3NT
♡ 10 5 4	♡ A Q		
◇ K 4 2	◇ 6 5 3		
♣ K Q 7 2	♣ A J 10 9 8		

North leads the ♡ 2 and you are immediately faced with the dilemma of whether to settle for your nine top tricks or try the heart finesse for an overtrick, risking defeat if South takes the ♡ K and switches to a diamond. Playing rubber bridge, or teams of four, where overtricks are of little consequence compared to the safety of your contract, you would be crazy to risk defeat. In pairs play there are a number of factors that make it correct to finesse the ♡ Q.

i) You are in a normal contract, and as most pairs will also be playing the weak no trump there is no reason to doubt that West will always be declarer. Therefore the number of tricks made will be the factor that determines who scores well.

ii) The ♡ 2 may not have been an obvious lead as it is plain that North has only four hearts. It is possible that other declarers may have been favoured with a diamond lead, giving an easy ten tricks.

iii) By finessing, you are far more likely to make an overtrick (50%) than fail (at worst 25%, when *both* finesses fail *and* South finds the diamond switch at trick 2).

iv) Even if both red suit finesses are wrong South is quite likely to misread the position and return his partner's suit.

Nonetheless, you should not automatically chase overtricks.

West	East	West	East
♠ A K Q	♠ 8 5 2	1♡	2◇
♡ A 9 6 5	♡ 8 3 2	3NT	
◇ 8 4	◇ A K Q 5 3		
♣ A 4 3 2	♣ 9 7		

In this example you take the ♠ J lead with your ♠ A and count eight top tricks. Again you seem to be in a normal contract. If the diamonds break 3-3 you can take ten tricks, but that will only happen 36% of the time. It is clearly correct to safeguard your contract against the more likely 4-2 diamond break by ducking a diamond at trick 2. Exchange East's ♡ 2 for the ◇ 2 and it would be reasonable to aim for eleven tricks by cashing East's diamond winners from the top. The difference is that if you are missing only five diamonds the chances of a favourable split have risen to 68%.

Sometimes you can judge that one off will give you a respectable score, even though you bid freely to your contract. In the example below North leads the ♡ K.

West	East	West	East
♠ K 4 3 2	♠ A Q 8	1NT	3NT
♡ A 7	♡ 8 3		
♢ K Q J 3	♢ 10 5 4 2		
♣ 6 4 3	♣ A K 10 9		

The bidding and lead both seem normal, so you are not at a disadvantage compared to other pairs. Let us assume the heart suit is breaking 5-4. You can make your contract if North has the ♣ Q J and spades break 3-3, but if you finesse the ♣ 10 by far the most likely result is two off as the defenders take one club, the ♢ A and four hearts. If you settle for one off by driving out the ♢ A you will be in good company!

On the other hand, suppose you take the same example, with the same bidding sequence, but this time your ♢ K is replaced by the ♢ 9. You miscounted your points as dealer and are in a dreadful, and abnormal, contract. Two off is most unlikely to be a success, and your only chance of a respectable score is to stake everything on an even spade break and North holding a favourable club position. Certainly if you make 3NT you can expect a top!

Quiz Plan each of these contracts:
a) playing rubber bridge   b) playing duplicate pairs

1)	♠ A K Q 10 9 8	♠ J 6	West	East
	♡ 9	♡ A 7 6 4 2	2♠	2NT
	♢ A K 4 2	♢ 6 3	3♢	3♠
	♣ 9 5	♣ J 4 3 2	4♠	

North leads the ♡ K.

2)   ♠ A K J 3   ♠ 8 4   West   East
    ♡ J 10 3 2   ♡ 9 8 4   1NT   3NT
    ◇ 3 2   ◇ A K Q 10 7 5
    ♣ A 8 3   ♣ 7 2

North leads the ♠ 2 to South's ♠ 9 and your ♠ J.

3)   ♠ A 10 4   ♠ K J 6   West   East
    ♡ A 10 9 6 3   ♡ K Q 7 5 2   1♡   4NT
    ◇ 9 3   ◇ A Q   5♠   5NT
    ♣ A 10 2   ♣ K Q 3   6♣   6♡

North leads the ♣ 8.

4)   ♠ K 6   ♠ A 5   West   East
    ♡ J 10 6 5   ♡ K Q 9   1NT   3NT
    ◇ A K Q 10   ◇ J 8 3
    ♣ 7 4 3   ♣ K Q J 5 2

North leads the ♠ Q.

5)   ♠ K 5 3   ♠ 9 4 2   West   East
    ♡ K 7 3 2   ♡ A 8 4   1NT   3NT
    ◇ A K 5 2   ◇ Q J 6 3
    ♣ 8 5   ♣ A K Q

North leads the ♡ 5.

Answers to quiz
1) a) Win the ♡ A, take your ◇ A, and duck a diamond, a
     safety play against a 6-1 break. Later ruff the ◇ 4 with the
     ♠ J.
  b) 4♠ seems a normal contract so overtricks will be import-
     ant. Take your ◇ A K and ruff the ◇ 4 with the ♠ 6,
     aiming for 11 tricks.

2) a) Lead the ◇ 2 to dummy's ◇ 7. This guarantees the
     contract unless South has all five missing diamonds.
  b) Finesse the ◇ 10. This reduces your chances of an over-
     trick from over 70% to 50%, but things are going so well it
     is worth a small insurance policy. Some pairs won't be in
     3NT, others might have a less favourable lead.

3) a) Draw trumps, eliminate clubs, and play ◇ A and ◇ Q. Whoever takes the ◇ K will be endplayed.

   b) The same. Why take a 25% risk of going down in your slam for only a 25% chance of an overtrick?

4) a) Take the ♠ A and drive out the ♡ A to ensure nine tricks.

   b) Aim for ten tricks by winning the ♠ K and leading towards dummy's club suit. If the ♣ K wins the trick try the ♡ 9, overtaking with the ♡ 10! If that also wins switch back to clubs, giving you a chance of eleven tricks! Of course, if South has ♣ A 10 x x you will be defeated, but you are in a normal contract and must take the line of play that will usually achieve an overtrick.

5) a) Take the ♡ A and cash your nine top tricks to ensure the contract!

   b) Take the ♡ A and finesse the ♠ K. Yes, you do risk defeat, but this type of barefaced nerve is safer than it seems. Even if North has the ♠ A the suit is likely to break 4-3, and if South does have ♠ Q J x x x, North may have seen no reason not to persevere with a heart. Even better he may duck with ♠ A x x, hoping that you hold ♠ K Q 10 and misguess on the next round.

13. Declarer Play if Progress Differs from Other Tables

We now develop the theme of how to react if you judge that the hand is progressing differently from the rest of the room. This was briefly mentioned at the start of chapter 12.

Keeping ahead of the field

You may judge your progress to be ahead of the field either as a result of the bidding, in which you have bid to a favourable contract that you expect other pairs to miss, or as a result of a lucky opening lead, or misdefence by your opponents.

Consider your declarer play as West in this example if North leads the ♣ 2.

West	East	West	East
♠ K Q J 8 7 4	♠ A 6 5 3 2	1♠	4◇ (1)
♡ A	♡ 9 7 5 4	4♡ (2)	6♠
◇ 9 6	◇ —		
♣ 10 7 6 3	♣ A Q J 8		

(1) 4◇ is a splinter bid showing excellent spade support and a singleton or void diamond.
(2) 4♡ is a cue bid showing the ♡ A or void and slam interest.

Your use of splinter bids and excellent judgement has enabled you to reach a fine slam with only 21 HCP. Most declarers will be in 4♠, so you are assured of at least an 80% score for making 6♠. However if you take the club finesse at trick 1, South winning the ♣ K and giving North a ruff, you will score a round zero! This is emphatically *not* the time to chase overtricks. Take your ♣ A and draw trumps.

By way of contrast, in the next example you judge yourself favourably placed partly by your partner's choice of contract, and partly by the opening lead.

West	East	West	East
♠ 4 3 2	♠ A 8		1♡
♡ Q J 8	♡ A K 10 9 7 2	1NT	3NT
◇ 5 4 3 2	◇ A Q 6		
♣ K 8 4	♣ 7 6		

North leads the ♣ 3 to South's ♣ 10 and your ♣ K. It seems that North has the ♣ A and you have been given an undeserved trick by the opening lead. Those who are in 4♡ will surely fail, losing a spade, two clubs and at least one diamond. Therefore settle for your nine tricks, confident that you will get an excellent score.

The next example looks similar at first sight, but appearances can be deceptive!

West	East	West	East
♠ 4 3 2	♠ A 8		1♡
♡ Q J 8	♡ A K 10 9 7 2	1NT	3NT
◇ 5 4 3 2	◇ A Q J		
♣ A 8 4	♣ 7 6		

Again the ♣ 3 is led, but don't expect nine tricks to score well this time! The field in 4♡ will make at least ten tricks, eleven if the diamond finesse works, and twelve if diamonds also break 3-3. If the diamond finesse fails you are in trouble, but if it works you should get as many tricks as those pairs who have chosen to play in a heart contract, earning you a top! Don't duck more than one club in case twelve tricks are thus available, use the heart entries to your hand to finesse diamonds twice, and finally re-enter your hand for the thirteenth diamond if it is by then a winner.

Catching up the field

Desperate measures to recover lost ground may be necessary after bidding to a poor contract, or as a result of an unlucky opening lead.

Try your judgement with the next example. After some thought North leads the ♣ 2 to South's ♣ A, the ♣ 3 is returned to North's ♣ K, and dummy's ♣ J wins trick 3.

West	East	West	East
♠ A J 6 5 4	♠ K 8 7 3	1♠	3♠
♡ K 2	♡ A 9 7 6 3	4♠	
◇ A K Q 4	◇ 9		
♣ Q 8	♣ J 10 9		

The bidding was normal, but North has found a successful attacking lead away from his ♣ K. On any other lead you could have thrown two of dummy's clubs on your diamond winners, therefore you are heading for a poor score. Your best chance of regaining lost ground is to cash dummy's ♠ K and finesse your ♠ J. Taken in isolation, this play is marginally inferior to playing for the ♠ Q to drop under the ♠ A on the second round, but you need to take a line which is *different* from the rest of the field!

Incidentally, even if you believe that other pairs are likely to be in 6♠ that should not affect your play as you cannot influence your score relative to them. If they succeed they will beat you whatever you do. If they fail, you will beat them!

Here is another example:

West	East	West	East
♠ Q J 7 5 2	♠ A K 8 6 4 3	1♠	3♣
♡ A K 10 3	♡ Q 8	3♡	3♠
♢ 4 3	♢ K 7	4♠	
♣ 9 5	♣ A 6 2		

North leads the ♢ Q to dummy's ♢ K and South's ♢ A, and wins trick 2 with the ♢ 10 before switching to the ♣ 3. Not everybody will have opened with your hand and the normal contract will be 4♠ by *East*! The ♢ K will then be protected from the opening lead, and making 11 tricks will be easy as declarer can discard the ♢ 7 on dummy's third heart. To recover lost ground you must take your ♣ A, draw trumps, cash the ♡ Q, and finesse the ♡ 10, even though you risk being defeated in a laydown contract! If South has the ♡ J you will be able to discard both of dummy's club losers, hopefully equalling the rest of the field who will be making eleven tricks by more orthodox methods! Note that if the defender with the ♡ J has it guarded no more than twice, you have no hope of catching those declaring 4♠ from the East hand. They will all make twelve tricks by discarding two of their losers on hearts.

However, this similar-looking example is very different!

West	East	West	East
♠ A K 7 5 2	♠ Q J 8 6 4 3	1♠	4♠
♡ K Q 10 3	♡ A 8		
♢ 4 3	♢ K 7		
♣ 9 5	♣ A 6 2		

The defence is identical but this time you have no reason to believe that things are any different elsewhere. The contract and declarer are normal, and a diamond lead from ♢ Q J 10 seems clearcut. Unless you are desperate enough for a top to risk a bottom, draw trumps and cash your ♡ A K Q, settling for ten tricks unless the ♡ J falls.

Quiz   Plan your play with these hands at *Love all*.

1) ♠ 6   ♠ A 5 3 2   West   East
    ♡ 10 9 3 2   ♡ —   3♣   6♣
    ◇ 10 5   ◇ A K Q J 6 3
    ♣ A K 8 7 6 4 ♣ 5 3 2

North leads the ♡ A.

2) ♠ K Q J 7 6   ♠ 10 9 8 5   West   East
    ♡ 2   ♡ A Q J   1♠   3♠
    ◇ A K Q J   ◇ 10 4 2   4♠
    ♣ 9 8 5   ♣ A 7 6

After some thought, North leads the ♣ 2.

3) ♠ K 7 6 4   ♠ A Q J 5   West   East
    ♡ Q J 4   ♡ 6 5 3 2   1NT   2♣
    ◇ A K 9   ◇ J 8   2♠   3♠
    ♣ 8 7 4   ♣ A 6 5

North leads his singleton ♡ 7, and collects a third round
ruff. He then switches to the ♣ K.

4) ♠ A K   ♠ 10 7   West   East
    ♡ 8 5 4   ♡ K 10 3   2NT   3NT
    ◇ K 10 3   ◇ A Q J 9 4
    ♣ A K Q J 10   ♣ 9 4 3

After some thought North leads the ♡ 2.

5) ♠ 7 5 4 3   ♠ 8 6   West   East
    ♡ K Q 9 7   ♡ J 10 8   1♡   2♡
    ◇ A K 3   ◇ 8 2
    ♣ K 2   ♣ A 8 7 6 5 3

North leads a trump to South's ♡ A and a trump is returned.

6) ♠ A K J 8   ♠ 10 9 6 2   West   East
    ♡ A K 3   ♡ Q J   1♠   2♠
    ◇ J 6 5   ◇ A K 2
    ♣ 6 4 3   ♣ 9 8 5 2

North leads the ♣ K Q, followed by the ♣ J to South's
♣ A. South exits with the ♡ 10.

7) ♠ A 3   ♠ 8 4   West   East
    ♡ K J 10 7   ♡ Q 9 8   1♢   2♢
    ♢ K J 10 3 2   ♢ A Q 6 4   2♡   4♡
    ♣ A K   ♣ 9 4 3 2

You take North's ♠ K lead with the ♠ A and play two rounds of trumps without the ace being taken.

8) ♠ A Q 6 5 4   ♠ J 10 9 7 3   West   East
    ♡ 10 9 4   ♡ K J   1♠   3♠
    ♢ A K Q   ♢ 7 6   4♠
    ♣ K 2   ♣ A 9 8 7

North leads the ♡ 2, South taking dummy's ♡ J with the ♡ Q and returning the ♡ 3 to North's ♡ A. North exits with the ♢ 3.

9) ♠ A K J 6 5   ♠ Q 10 9 8 7   West   East
    ♡ A   ♡ Q   1♠   4♠
    ♢ Q J 5   ♢ 10 9 6
    ♣ J 10 9 4   ♣ A K 5 3

North leads the ♢ K, followed by the ♢ 2 to South's ♢ A, and North ruffs the third round, exiting with ♡ K.

Answers to quiz

1) You are in an excellent contract, made easy after your slightly offbeat pre-emptive opening bid. Since most pairs are unlikely to proceed beyond game you will undoubtedly score well by making your slam, therefore you must take the safety play that safeguards your contract against a 3-1 trump break. Trump the ♡ A and duck a trump.

2) It seems that the damaging club lead was not clearcut, so many declarers in this standard contract will have an easy path to eleven tricks. You would like to combine the need for an overtrick with safety by taking a ruffing heart finesse, but you don't have a quick re-entry to dummy. Therefore enter your hand with the ♢ A and finesse the ♡ Q.

3) With 25 HCP most pairs will probably be in 3NT going one off, or 4♠ going two off. Therefore you should settle for one off, rather than desperately trying a double finesse to set up a diamond discard for one of your losing clubs.

4) As the hearts seem to be breaking 4-3 your 3NT is not in danger, so do you give yourself a chance of 13 tricks by rising with the ♡ K, or settle for a safe 11 tricks by playing dummy's ♡ 10? Firstly, you cannot influence your score compared to those in a slam, so forget them. You must aim to beat those in 3NT, and since some will not have received a heart lead they will find an easy route to 12 tricks. 13 tricks will undoubtedly score well, but the difference between 9 and 11 will be slight, so try the ♡ K.

5) You have two options here. If trumps break 3-3 and clubs 3-2 you can cash the ♣ K A, ruff a club high, enter dummy with the ♡ J and make ten tricks. Alternatively, you can guarantee eight tricks by ruffing the ◇ 3 in dummy, re-entering your hand with the ♣ K, and drawing trumps. The key is that 110 is likely to score well. Those in 1NT will probably score only 90, those in clubs at most 110, and if East/West protect they are unlikely to lose more than 100 in 2♠ or 3◇. Therefore choose the second option.

6) Again forget those pairs in 4♠. If it fails you are bound to score well whatever you do, while if it makes you will score badly. The only thing you can control is your score compared to any other pairs in a spade part-score, and to that effect you must play the trump suit normally by taking a second round finesse of the ♠J.

7) Don't play a third round of trumps and risk being forced if they break 4-2! Just play diamonds until somebody ruffs. That way you guarantee to restrict your losers to two trumps and one spade, scoring 420. Some pairs will be in 3NT going off on the ♠ K lead, and others in 5◇ will be held to 400. Therefore 420 will be an excellent score, and it would be foolish to risk defeat in a greedy chase for 450.

8) You are in a normal contract, but surely few other Norths will have underled the ♡ A! Without a heart lead you could easily dispose of a heart loser on the ◇ Q, therefore you are a trick behind the room. Your only chance of recovery is in the trump suit, so you must spurn the finesse and try to drop the ♠ K singleton offside.

9) Another obvious contract, and again a far from obvious opening lead has put you a trick behind the room. You must try to recover in the club suit, spurning the finesse and hoping to drop the ♣ Q doubleton offside.

14. Gracefully Accepting Defeat

West	East
♠ A 9 7	♠ 8 4
♡ Q 7 3	♡ K 8 4 2
◇ 9 7 5	◇ J 10 6
♣ K Q J 4	♣ A 7 6 2

i)

South	West	North	East
		1♠	No
No	1NT	No	No
No			

ii)

South	West	North	East
		1♠	No
No	1NT	Double	No
No	No		

After either auction, you duck North's ♠ K lead and ♠ Q continuation, taking the ♠ A at trick 3. From South's signals spades appear to be breaking 5-3. How many tricks do you need in 1NT, or 1NT doubled, for a good score? Although your protective 1NT was reasonable no doubt some Wests will have chosen to let the bidding die, allowing North/South to make a likely 140 in 1♠. Thus, not for the first time, −100 is likely to give you a good score, but −200 or even −150 will score poorly. You have two choices.

i) You can lead up to the ♡ K. If this works you will escape for one off, but if North takes his ♡ A, North/South will probably also come to four spades and four diamonds.

ii) You can cash your four club tricks before leading a heart. This will restrict your losses to two off, but your chances of sneaking through a heart will have been severely damaged as the defenders will be able to exchange signals.

The dilemma is resolved by your need to escape for −100. If you are not vulnerable and auction i) has occurred, cash your clubs. On the other hand if you are vulnerable, or you have been doubled as in auction ii), try a heart.

Sacrifice contracts

If you have sacrificed over an enemy contract you must keep in mind the score against which you have sacrificed.

West	East	South	West	North	East
♠ K Q 10 9 7	♠ J 8 6 3	1♡	1♠	4♡	4♠
♡ 8 4 2	♡ 3	Double	No	No	No
◇ A Q	◇ 8 6 3 2				
♣ 9 4 3	♣ 10 6 5 2				

South overtakes North's ♡ Q lead with his ♡ K and leads the ♠ A, followed by the ♠ 2, North discarding a heart. At trick 3 you ruff a heart, and exit from dummy with a diamond. If you finesse the ◇ Q you will end up with eight tricks if it wins, but only six if North has the ◇ K as South may gain the lead with a club and remove dummy's last trump. On the other hand if you rise with the ◇ A, another heart ruff will ensure seven tricks. The key is the vulnerability. At *Love all* there is no point in sacrificing against 450 or 480, only to concede 500. You need 8 tricks (−300) to make your sacrifice worthwhile so finesse the ◇ Q. However at *Green* vulnerability −500 should score well against −620 or −650, so take the ◇ A.

It is also worth considering whether the contract against which you have sacrificed would have succeeded!

West	East		*North/South Game*		
♠ A 9 8 7 5 3	♠ K J 2	South	West	North	East
♡ −	♡ A K			1♡	No
◇ J 10 9 8	◇ 7 5 4 3	4♡	4♠	Double	No
♣ 7 4 3	♣ 8 6 5 2	No	No		

North cashes the ◇ A K Q, switches to the ♣ Q which holds, and then South takes the ♣ A K, exiting with a heart. This is not a sacrifice you expect the rest of the room to find, and you will lose 500 or 800 depending on the trump position. The important thing is to try to keep your losses to 500 (below their vulnerable game); *when 4♡ is making*, i.e., when spades are 3-1. Therefore cash your ♠ A and finesse the ♠ J.

The role of counting

It is impossible to do justice to the theme of declarer counting in this book, but just one example will demonstrate how keeping your wits about you can help you to place vital missing cards. North leads the ◇ A K and switches to the ♠ 6.

West	East	South	West	North	East
♠ 4 3	♠ K J 5 2			1◇	No
♡ K 3	♡ 6 5 4	1♡	2♣	2♡	3♣
◇ Q 8 2	◇ J 6	No	No	No	
♣ A J 8 7 4 3	♣ K Q 10 9				

When both defenders have entered the auction counting points is usually quite easy, so we must gather the evidence. You are missing 20 HCP, and North seems to have 13 or 14. Since he has turned up with 7 diamond points it is very likely that the two major suit aces are in separate hands so you have two options.

i) Try to make your contract. You will require South to have the ♡ A so North will have to hold the ♠ A. Should you follow this line of thought and rise with the ♠ K you will go two off if you are wrong.

ii) Give yourself the best chance of one off. You can never go more than one off if South has the ♡ A, so assume North has it. Therefore South has the ♠ A, so try the ♠ J.

It is likely that your opponents can make 3♡, indeed it is quite extraordinary that they have allowed you to play in 3♣! Therefore −100 could be a good score, particularly since not every West will enter the auction. This suggests that if you are vulnerable option ii) is best, avoiding the dreaded −200. Incidentally, North's most likely reason for not switching to his partnership's agreed suit at trick 3 is that he has the unsupported ace! If you are not vulnerable the difference between −50 and −100 is likely to be negligible, so option i) wins the vote.

Quiz

West	East
1) ♠ J 7 6 5 4	♠ 10 9 3
♡ 7 6 4	♡ 10 8
◇ A K Q	◇ 8 6 5 4
♣ 6 5	♣ A K J 7

	Game all					*Love all*		
i)	South	West	North	East	ii)	South	West	North	East
	1♡	No	1NT	No		1♡	No	1NT	No
	2♡	2♠	No	No		2♡	2♠	No	No
	No					3♡	No	No	3♠
						Dblc	No	No	No

North leads a spade and South takes the ♠ A Q before switching to the ◇ J. When you cash the ◇ A K Q you discover that North started with four. Plan the play:
    a) after auction i).   b) after auction ii).
    c) after auction ii) without the double.

2) West	East	South	West	North	East
♠ A Q 10 9 7	♠ K J 8 6 5 2	3♡	3♠	4NT	6♠
♡ Q	♡ J 9 3	No	No	Dble	No
◇ Q J 10 9	◇ −	No	No		
♣ 8 5 3	♣ 10 7 4 2				

North leads the ♠ 4, South following suit with the ♠ 3. Plan the play:
a) at *Love all*.   b) at *Green* vulnerability.

3) West	East	South	West	North	East
♠ A Q 7 5 4 3	♠ K J 10 2	1NT(1)	2♠	No	No
♡ 8 3	♡ 9 7	No			
◇ 8 2	◇ K J 3				
♣ K 3 2	♣ 8 7 6 5	(1) 1NT shows 12-14 HCP			

North cashes the ♡ Q J and switches to the ◇ 4. Plan the play:
a) at *Love all*.   b) at *Game all*.

Answers to quiz

1) Some North/South pairs will play in 2♡. They can certainly make 2♡, possibly 3♡, so −100 is likely to be reasonable but

−200 or −300 a disaster. Therefore:
  a) and c) Don't finesse the ♣ J. Settle for −100.
  b) Finesse the ♣ J. −500 won't be much worse than −300.

2) The bidding suggests that North may have the ♢ A K, but
   you cannot be certain. You have two options:
     i) Lead the ♢ Q ruffing out North's ♢ A, return to your
     hand and take a ruffing finesse against the ♢ K. If North
     has both diamond honours you will discard two of
     dummy's clubs, losing only 300. If South has the ♢ A or
     ♢ K you will concede 700.
     ii) Take no risks. If North fails to cover your ♢ Q ruff all
     your diamonds in dummy, settling for a safe −500.
       Perhaps 6♡ would have gone off, but it is too late to
     worry about that! Some North/South pairs will play in 4♡,
     so you must aim to beat them. Therefore:
   a) Aim for −300 with option i), aiming to beat −420.
   b) −500 is OK as they can make 620, so settle for option ii).

3) −100 will clearly give you an excellent score as it is plain that
   your cheeky two-level overcall prevented opponents finding
   a heart fit that would have netted them at least 140. You
   are missing 23 HCP, and it seems that South started with the
   ♡ A K, so he cannot have both minor suit aces! It is just
   possible that North has both of them, but in all probability
   they are divided. Therefore:
   a) At *Love all* you might as well try to make your contract,
      just in case some North/South pairs are failing in 4♡. Rise
      with the ♢ K, playing for North to have the ♢ A and
      South the ♣ A. If you go two off you should still score
      well.
   b) At *Game all*, aim for one off. Assume that North has the
      ♣ A, so South has the ♢ A. Therefore try the ♢ J.

Part 4   Defensive Play

15. Defensive Counting

When you first investigated the mysteries of bridge you learned to defend by 'rules'. 'Second hand plays low', 'Third hand plays high', 'Cover an honour with an honour', and woe betide the retrograde who dares not to return his partner's suit. Of course, there is a lot of truth in these rules, at least in the early tricks of the defence if there is not much evidence to guide you. But it doesn't take much imagination to think of examples when blind obedience to a rule is idiotic. For example, if declarer wins your opening lead against 4♡ and leads the ♣ 2 through your ♣ A towards dummy's ♣ K J you would be wise to duck and hope the ♣ J loses to the ♣ Q. Supposing the same play happened later in the hand when you have already come to three tricks, partner will not be too impressed if you duck and never make your ♣ A!

These rules should be given their proper role in defence: namely, guidelines until logical analysis provides a better answer. To argue logically you need access to information which comes from a number of sources: partner's or opponents' bidding, partner's signalling, or simply reasoning that declarer's play only makes sense if he has, or is missing, a certain card. The difficult part is gathering this information together, and processing it in your mind. It certainly requires a considerable feat of concentration when you first attempt it, but becomes much easier with practice. The gathering of the information is called *counting*. The reasoning can then be divided into two categories.

Firstly, there is the argument 'I have enough information to establish that partner has this vital card'.

Secondly, there is the logic which states 'I can't be sure whether or not partner has this card, but I do know that unless he has it declarer is bound to succeed, therefore I will assume partner has it.'

The first line of reasoning is crucial in any form of bridge, but particularly so in duplicate pairs where preventing overtricks, or getting declarer that extra one off, can be vitally important.

The second argument tends to be more dangerous at pairs scoring because you usually cannot afford to throw away overtricks in the vain hope that partner has the one card that will defeat the contract. Nevertheless, there are certain circumstances when you can tell that you are bound to get a poor score unless you defeat the contract. Perhaps you have doubled it, or you can tell that your opponents have found a particularly good contract that the rest of the room will miss, or you have already given away a trick with a less than clearcut opening lead.

Counting points

Counting points tends to be particularly profitable if one of these conditions applies:

i) Declarer, or your partner, has made a limit bid during the auction.

ii) Declarer, or your partner, has passed during the auction but has shown up with a number of high cards on the first few tricks.

Here is a typical example of systematic counting, followed by logical analysis.

♠ A 7 3
♡ Q 8 5
◇ J 6 4 2
♣ A Q J

North/South Game
Dealer East

♠ 9 8 6 2
♡ K J 9 3
◇ K 10 9
♣ 8 4

South	West	North	East
			No
No	No	1 ◇(1)	No
3NT	No	No	No

(1) North/South are playing the strong no trump.

West (your partner) leads the ♠ Q, taken by South's ♠ K. Declarer continues by playing a club to dummy's ♣ Q, successfully finesses the ◇ Q in his hand, cashes the ◇ A and ducks a diamond to your ◇ K, partner following suit. What now? If you have been keeping count of declarer's points you can place every vital card. He has shown up with the ♠ K, and ◇ A Q. This gives him 9 HCP. However, despite his leap to 3NT, *he had already passed!* Therefore he cannot have the ♡ A, so presumably he must have the ♣ K. It is hearts, not spades, that will be your source of tricks so you should be prepared to find the killing switch to your ♡ 3, enabling you to take your four heart tricks. His hand could well be:

♠ K 5 4   ♡ 10 7 2   ◇ A Q 3   ♣ K 10 6 3

The heart switch, which looks dangerous on superficial analysis, is quite safe unless declarer unaccountably passed as dealer with 13 HCP. Playing pairs you tend to defend passively, avoiding underleading honours, but that is not an excuse for mental laziness if you have the clues that indicate the winning defence. Perhaps you don't like South's bidding, leaping to 3NT after a fourth in hand 1◇ opening. That is irrelevant. Playing duplicate pairs you must take advantage of opponents' indiscretions, not criticize them.

Counting shape

When the bidding, or partner's signals combined with the cards already played, give you a count in three suits it is possible to work out the distribution of the fourth suit.

♠ 6 4
♡ K 4 2
◇ A 8 7   *Game all*
♣ A 6 5 4 3   Dealer South

	♠ A 5 3	South	West	North	East
N	♡ A 7 5	1♡	No	2♣	No
W E	◇ 6 4 3	2◇	No	3♡	No
S	♣ K 10 8 2	3NT	No	No	No

Partner leads the ♠ 2 and your ♠ A holds the first trick. Would you believe that you already have enough information to work out declarer's exact shape? He has four spades (partner's ♠ 2 must be from a four-card holding, leaving declarer with four also), four hearts (with five he would have raised 3♡ to 4♡), four diamonds (with five he would presumably have opened 1◇), and therefore one club! Armed with that knowledge you must switch to the ♣ K in case declarer has the ♣ Q singleton.

He can make at most 3 spades, 4 diamonds and the ♣ A before you take 3 clubs and the two major suit aces. Perhaps declarer's hand is:

♠ K Q 10 7   ♡ Q J 10 6   ◇ K Q J 5   ♣ Q

Note that the ♣ K switch, which seems so dangerous if declarer might have a holding like ♣ Q J 7, is totally safe; indeed a perfect pairs play! Once again, automatically returning your partner's suit is not necessarily correct.

Counting tricks

♠ Q J 7
♡ A K Q
◇ A K J 10
♣ Q 6 2

Love all
Dealer South

	♠ 8 2	South	West	North	East
N	♡ 9 6 3	2♠ (1)	No	4NT (2)	No
W **E**	◇ 9 4 2	5◇ (2)	No	6♠	No
S	♣ K 10 9 8 3	No	No		

(1) 2♠ shows 6-10 points and 6 spades.
(2) 4NT is Blackwood and 5◇ shows one ace.

After this somewhat crude sequence in which North didn't seem unduly worried whether or not there were two club losers, West leads the ♡ J. Dummy takes the ♡ A, leads the ♠ Q to partner's ♠ A, takes the heart exit with the ♡ K and draws the last trumps with the ♠ J. Now he leads dummy's ♣ Q. If you automatically cover an honour with an honour that will be the end for the defence. Declarer's 5◇ reply to Blackwood shows the ♣ A, and leading the ♣ Q only makes sense if he has the ♣ J. However if he had twelve *sure* tricks he would hardly be taking a finesse, so by now you can diagnose his problem. He has eleven certain tricks, 5 spades, 3 hearts, 2 diamonds and the ♣ A, so he is missing the ◇ Q and has a choice of finesses for his contract. Duck the ♣ Q quickly and if it is your lucky day he will rise with the ♣ A and take an unsuccessful ruffing finesse in diamonds. At least give him the chance to go wrong! He probably has:

♠ K 10 9 6 4 3   ♡ 7 5 2   ◇ 8 5   ♣ A J

In fact declarer has insulted you by adopting this line. His percentage play is to try to ruff out the ◇ Q, and then take the club finesse. He has preferred to assume that you will naively give the game away, so your pride is at stake here!

Combining your counting

So far you have seen one example each of counting points, shape and tricks. Of course, frequently you must keep count of more than one of these.

♠ 9 4
♡ A K J 10
◇ 6 3
♣ K Q J 10 8

	♠ Q J 7			
	♡ 8 6 3 2			
	◇ K Q 4			
	♣ A 7 6			

Love all
Dealer North

South	West	North	East
		1♣	No
2NT	No	3NT	No
No	No		

Partner leads the ♠ 3 to your ♠ J. This holds the trick, as does your ♠ Q continuation, West contributing the ♠ 2. Before mindlessly leading a third spade pause and think! You have 12 HCP, dummy has 14 and declarer has promised 11-12. Partner can have at most three, obviously the ♠ K as he started with five spades. Therefore he has no entry for his spade suit. Turning your attention to counting tricks, declarer clearly has ten if given time (the ♠ A, ◇ A, 4 hearts and 4 clubs) so a diamond switch is called for.

It is here that pairs thinking differs from rubber bridge. Playing rubber bridge you should reason that the only chance of defeating the contract is to underlead your ◇ K Q and hope that declarer misguesses with ◇ A J 9. When playing pairs that policy is all too likely to force declarer into a play that will give him ten tricks; for example if he holds ◇ A J 10 or ◇ A J 2 he will have no choice but to try the ◇ J! In a moderate field you should reason that you are already ahead of the field. Declarer is in a normal contract and your partner has chosen to underlead a single honour in his five-card suit without an outside entry, getting the defence off to a flying start. Even if other Wests find the spade lead, not every East will have the presence of mind to switch suit, so lead the ♢ K and settle for four tricks.

Quiz

In this quiz partner can be relied upon to lead his fourth-highest card, but doesn't play any length signals or the improved system of leads described in chapters 17 and 18. Of course, if your signalling system improves, good defending becomes even easier!

1)

	♠ K Q 10 9	
	♡ K 10 9 2	
	♢ A 4	*Love all*
	♣ K Q 9	Dealer South

♠ 8 6 4			*South*	*North*
♡ 8 6	N		1♡	4NT
♢ K Q J 2	W E		5♠ (1)	6♡
♣ A 4 3 2	S			

(1) 5♠ shows two aces and the ♡ Q

You confidently lead the ♢ K against 6♡, taken by dummy's ♢ A. Declarer then draws two rounds of trumps, partner following to both, cashes 4 spades discarding a diamond, and ruffs the ♢ 4. He now leads a club to dummy's ♣ K, returns to his hand with a trump and leads another club. How do you defend?

2) ♠ A K 6 5 4
♡ 9
♢ A K Q 10
♣ K J 10

			Love all	
N	♠ 3 2		Dealer North	
W E	♡ A Q 10		*South*	*North*
S	♢ J 5 4 2			1♠
	♣ A 4 3 2		1NT	3♢
			3NT	

Partner's ♠ Q wins trick 1, and declarer takes the ♠ J continuation with dummy's ♠ A, discarding the ♢ 6 from his hand. Dummy's ♣ K is then called for. If you duck, clubs will be continued. Plan the defence.

3)

```
            ♠ K Q 10 4
            ♡ A Q 8
            ♢ K 9          Love all
            ♣ A K 3 2      Dealer South
♠ 9 2           ┌─────┐    South    North
♡ J 10 9        │  N  │    1♠       3♣
♢ Q 8 4 2       │W   E│    3♠       4NT
♣ J 6 5 4       │  S  │    5♡ (1)   5NT
                └─────┘    6♢ (2)   7♠
            (1) two aces  (2) one king
```

Your ♡ J lead is won by dummy's ♡ A. Declarer plays 5 rounds of trumps, the ♡ K and ♡ Q. You must find 3 minor suit discards.

4)

```
            ♠ A K Q 9 8
            ♡ A 3
            ♢ A K          Love all
            ♣ A 10 9 8     Dealer West
♠ 7             ┌─────┐    South West North East
♡ K Q J 9 8 7 5 │  N  │         3♡   4♡    No
♢ 8 6 3         │W   E│    4♠   No   5♣    No
♣ J 4           │  S  │    6♠   No   No    No
                └─────┘
```

Your ♡ K lead is taken by dummy's ♡ A. Declarer than calls for the ♠ A K, drawing two trumps from partner, cashes the ♢ A K, and exits with the ♡ 3 to your ♡ K, East again following suit. How do you continue the defence?

5)

```
            ♠ Q J 10 8
            ♡ A J 9
            ♢ K 5 4        Love all
            ♣ 7 5 3        Dealer South
♠ 9 5 3         ┌─────┐    South    North
♡ Q 3           │  N  │    1NT      2♣
♢ J 9 7 3 2     │W   E│    2♢       3NT
♣ A 6 2         │  S  │
                └─────┘
```

On your ♢ 3 lead, partner's ♢ 8 is taken by declarer's ♢ 10. At trick 2 the ♣ K is led. Plan the defence.

6)   ♠ 9 5 2
                      ♡ A Q 6
                      ♢ A Q 3 2   *North/South Game*
                      ♣ K 8 2   Dealer East

		South	West	North	East
♠ —	**N**				3♠
♡ K 10 9 7 5	**W** **E**				
♢ J 10 9 8 6	**S**	3NT	No	6NT	No
♣ 9 5 4		No	No		

Your ♢ J lead loses to declarer's ♢ K, partner discarding the
♠ 3. Declarer cashes four rounds of clubs (partner discarding
the ♠ 4 on the fourth and dummy jettisoning the ♠ 2) and
the ♠ A K. You discard the ♡ 5, ♡ 7 and ♢ 6. He continues
by taking dummy's ♢ A Q and throws you in with the ♢ 10.
You still have the ♡ K 10 9 and in dummy you can see the
♡ A Q 6. What next?

7) ♠ K Q 9
    ♡ 4 3 2
    ♢ Q J   *Game all*
    ♣ Q J 10 7 3   Dealer South

	♠ A J 10	South	North
N	♡ J 5	1♡	2♣
W **E**	♢ A K 6 2	2♠	3♡
S	♣ 9 8 4 2	4♡	

You take partner's ♢ 10 lead with the ♢ K and successfully
cash the ♢ A. Plan the defence.

Answers to quiz

1) Declarer started with 3 spades, 5 hearts, 2 diamonds, and
   therefore 3 clubs. If you play low your ♣ A cannot run away,
   and if declarer has the ♣ 10, but not the ♣ J, he might
   misguess.

2) Take the third club, cash the ♡ A, and exit with the ♢ 2.
   This gives a trick but declarer cannot reach his hand and is
   held to 8 tricks. Giving him access to his hand will concede at
   least two tricks, as he must have the ♡ K and ♣ Q. Of
   course, if declarer chooses to refuse your Trojan horse by
   taking your diamond exit with the ♢ A, you must be prepared to later jettison your ♢ J under the ♢ K or ♢ Q.

3) Count declarer's tricks; 5 spades, the ♡ A K Q, the ◇ A K and the ♣ A K. If he had a fourth heart it would be a winner, giving him thirteen easy tricks. Equally if he had a third diamond, a ruff in dummy would have provided the thirteenth trick. Therefore his shape must be 5-3-2-3. You can discard your diamonds, but you must keep at least 3 clubs to protect partner's ♣ Q x. Frequently the clues necessary for accurate counting are to be found in trying to make sense of declarer's play.

4) Declarer seems to have started with 5 spades and 2 hearts, leaving him with 6 minor suit cards.
   i) If he started with 4 diamonds and 2 clubs the defence will succeed if, and only if, East has the ♣ K. A diamond or club exit will be safe.
   ii) If he started with 3 diamonds and 3 clubs either the ♣ K or ♣ Q will suffice from partner, but you *must* exit with a diamond in case East started with ♣ Q 6 5 3.
   iii) If he started with 2 diamonds and 4 clubs, again the ♣ K or ♣ Q in partner's hand will be sufficient, provided you exit with a diamond or heart! The ruff and discard will only enable him to dispose of his *fourth* club.
   The exit card that caters for all these eventualities is the ◇ 8.

5) Declarer clearly has the ◇ A Q and his lead of the ♣ K suggests he also has the ♣ Q J. That makes 12 HCP, so East must have the ♠ A K and ♡ K. Given time declarer can undoubtedly score at least 6 minor suit tricks, the ♡ A and 2 spades so you must clearly switch to a heart. However the ♡ Q is not good enough, as North will rise with the ♡ A and you will never regain the lead to penetrate dummy's remaining ♡ J 9! If East has the ♡ 10 it is vital that you lead the ♡ 3, leaving declarer without resource.

6) If East has the ♡ J declarer has no chance. Conversely, if South has the ♡ J x x you are fatally endplayed. However if South has the ♡ J x and a spade you can foil him by exiting with the ♡ K. This gives him three tricks, but he is unable to unscramble his entries sufficiently to enjoy his winners.

7) For his reverse, declarer must have the ♡ A K Q and ♣ A K

as well as 5 hearts and 4 spades. But he followed suit to 2 diamonds, so the ♣ A K must be doubleton. This means he will have no access to dummy if you remove his spade entry! It looks unlikely, but switch to the ♠ J at trick 3, and then sit back patiently to collect two more spade tricks later!

16. General Defensive Duplicate Tactics

The greatest difference between defence at rubber bridge and duplicate pairs is the need for unflagging concentration. Unlike rubber bridge, when it is not unreasonable to relax a little when you have defeated declarer, or when you know he is bound to succeed, relaxing might cost an overtrick that determines whether or not you score well on the board! This makes high quality duplicate bridge far more stressful than rubber bridge for which the aims are usually far more clearcut.

As always, defensive technique consists of finding out what declarer is trying to do, and frustrating him. In this respect defending at duplicate pairs differs little from defending at rubber bridge, but pairs defending is complicated by the fact that you have no clear objectives. By rigorous counting you can sometimes build a full picture of the hand, but often the view is incomplete and you must take the percentage action. Generally speaking, you cannot stake everything on beating the contract as you might only succeed in presenting declarer with a crucial overtrick.

The opening lead

Playing pairs you should be more inclined to be passive than usual, avoiding leading from combinations that risk giving a trick unless the potential gain is substantial. If you are considering leading from a broken suit against no trumps, having a fifth card in the suit makes a world of difference. Leading from a four-card suit can only realistically establish one length trick, and then only if neither opponent has four. Holding five you have a far *better* chance of establishing *two* tricks as the other three players only have eight cards between them in the suit. Thus if your right-hand opponent's 1NT is passed out, lead the ♠ 4 from hand a), but a passive ♡ 8 from hand b). Leading from broken four-card suits is generally a mistake unless the bidding clearly pinpoints such a lead, or all the other possible leads are worse.

a) ♠ A J 6 4 3 ♡ 9 5   ◇ J 8 4 3   ♣ Q 9
b) ♠ K 8 6 4   ♡ 9 8 4 ◇ J 8 4 3   ♣ Q 9

You may even decide against leading from a good five-card suit if there is a safer alternative. Consider your lead as West with hand c) after auctions i) and ii).

c) ♠ 7 5 3   ♡ K J 10 4 3   ◇ Q 2   ♣ 7 5 3

i)	South	West	North	East	ii)	South	West	North	East
			1♠	No		2NT	No	No	No
	1NT	No	3NT	No					
	No	No							

After auction i) a heart lead is reasonable, *because the majority of the enemy strength is clearly concentrated in North's hand*. If North has the ♡ A Q 2 your attacking lead will have given declarer nothing that was not always rightfully his. After the bidding in ii), a heart lead is far too likely to find South with ♡ A Q 2. Not only will you then have thrown away a trick, but declarer will easily prevent you from establishing length tricks by ducking his ♡ A on the second round. The bidding marks East with at least 10 points, so wait for him to pierce declarer's heart holding. Having decided on a passive approach, a spade lead is slightly better than a club as with a borderline hand North would have been more inclined to proceed over 2NT with a major suit. Even if you had an outside entry I would not advise a heart lead; but change the ♡ K to the ♡ A and I would recommend the ♡ J (or ♡ 10, according to your methods.) This time your lead will not cost a trick if South has ♡ K Q 2, and furthermore your ♡ A gives you better control, preventing South from isolating your suit by ducking.

Against a suit contract a trump lead from a small doubleton or three small cards is often successful, combining a good chance of giving nothing away with the attacking potential of preventing ruffs in dummy.

Sometimes the bidding may cry out for an aggressive lead.

If you are East, on lead after this sequence, the bidding suggests that any trick you give away with an attacking lead is unlikely to help declarer! Unless you make an attacking lead declarer's diamond losers will disappear on dummy's heart suit! Lead the ♢ A from d) (otherwise he is all too likely to claim 13 tricks!) and the ♢ 2 from e), hoping partner has the ♢ A, or the ♢ Q and a heart or trump trick.

d) ♠ 7 5 3   ♡ 9 5 2   ♢ A 7 4 2   ♣ 10 3 2
e) ♠ 7 5 3   ♡ 9 5 2   ♢ K 7 4 2   ♣ 10 3 2

Estimating your progress against the room

Frequently you become aware that unless partner holds one specific card you cannot defeat the contract. Unfortunately playing duplicate pairs you usually dare not play on that assumption because it risks giving away overtricks. Sometimes you can tell that if declarer succeeds you are on course for a bad score, and you must aim therefore to beat the contract whatever the risks. This is often the case when declarer is clearly in a contract that is substantially different from the rest of the room. For example, perhaps your opponents were prepared to let the auction die in 3♡, but your protective 3♠ drove them into 4♡. You must now stake everything on beating them. Alternatively, they may have grotesquely underbid, as is shown in the next example.

♠ A J
♡ K 9 5 2
♢ J 10 9 4　　　*Love all*
♣ Q 10 8　　　Dealer South

♠ K Q 10 9　　　　South　North
♡ A 10 9 3　　　　　1♢　　　1♡
♢ K 6 3 2　　　　　1NT (1)　3♢
♣ 7

(1) 1NT shows 15-16 HCP

Your ♠ K lead is taken by dummy's ♠ A, and the ♢ J is run to your ♢ K. Unless you achieve something spectacular here you are heading for a very poor score. The clue is North's remarkable second bid. No doubt he thought it was forcing, but the result has been to keep North/South out of a 3NT contract that everybody else will bid. Since you can count five easy winners against 3NT (3 spades, the ♡ A and the ♢ K) you must assume that any plus score for North/South will give you a bottom. Have you any chance of defeating 3♢, bearing in mind that East can have at most two high card points? Only if he has exactly ♡ Q x, and you can engineer two heart tricks and a ruff. Cash your ♠ K and try the ♡ 3.

Incidentally, the desperate attempt to defeat 3♢ would be correct even if you thought 3NT was making, once you realised that everybody else would be defending a game contract. If the game makes it won't matter what you do, so your only chance to influence your fate is to assume 3NT will fail. In that case you need to beat 3♢ to stay level with the rest of the field. By all means *hope* that 3NT succeeds at other tables, but you must *play* on the assumption that it will fail.

In the previous example the bidding put you at a disadvantage compared to the rest of the room. This time your choice of opening lead causes the problem.

♠ K J 8 5
♡ A K
♢ J 9 8　　　*Love all*
♣ 10 9 8 7　　Dealer South

♠ 10 2　　　　South　West　North　East
♡ Q 10 6 4　　1NT　　No　　2♣　　No
♢ K Q 2　　　2♡　　　No　　3NT　　No
♣ A Q 4 2　　4♠　　　No　　No　　No

Faced with no particularly attractive lead you apprehensively decide upon the ♠ 2, and your worst fears are realised when declarer takes your partner's ♠ Q with his ♠ A and cashes dummy's ♠ K J, your partner following suit each time. Declarer then calls for dummy's ♣ 7 to his ♣ J and your ♣ Q. Your lead has plainly thrown away a trick, as declarer would presumably have finessed dummy's ♠ J without your help. Therefore you need to recover a trick. You know declarer started with four cards in each major, and his ♣ J suggests he started with a doubleton club, leaving him with three diamonds. Given time he will establish dummy's ♣ 10 9 for two diamond discards, therefore a diamond switch is plainly essential. The ◇ K will ensure three tricks for the defence, but that will be insufficient if other East/West pairs are making two clubs, a diamond, and the ♠ Q. To recover the ground you lost at trick 1 you must stake everything on East having the ◇ 10 and switch to the ◇ 2! Even if declarer has the ◇ 10 you can be sure that −450 will be not much worse than −420.

Cashing out

One of the unglamorous, but essential, skills of pairs is learning to recognise situations when your winners will evaporate unless you cash them quickly.

```
              ♠ A Q J
              ♡ 8 2
              ◇ Q 10 9 6 4 2      Love all
              ♣ J 7               Dealer South
♠ 10 9 8 7 6      N              South    North
♡ A Q 4 3      W     E           2NT      3NT
◇ A              S
♣ 9 5 2
```

Your ♠ 10 lead is won by declarer's ♠ K, and at trick 2 his ◇ K is taken by your ◇ A. Don't delude yourself that you can sit back and wait for two heart tricks! Declarer must have all the remaining HCP for his 2NT opening bid and you can count at least 11 tricks for him (3 spades, 5 diamonds and 3 clubs). This will become 12 if he has a fourth club so you can never expect more than one heart trick, and even this might vanish unless you cash it now!

Subterfuge

Occasionally you may be able to deflect declarer from successfully seeking overtricks by making him believe his contract is
at risk.

♠ J 10 9 8
♡ K Q
♢ A K Q 3 2   *Love all*
♣ 7 5   Dealer South

         ♠ Q 4 3   South   North
         ♡ 9 8 5 2   1NT   2♣
         ♢ J 5 4   2♠   4♠
         ♣ A 6 3

West cashes the ♣ K, and continues with the ♣ Q. By rights
that should be the last trick for the defence as declarer must have
the ♠ A K and ♡ A for his 1NT opening. You might be able to
deflect him from the trump finesse if you can persuade him that
he is in danger of conceding a ruff. Overtake the ♣ Q with the
♣ A and switch to the ♢ J. It might not work, but what can you
lose by trying? Holding 4♠ to ten tricks will undoubtedly give
you a top!

Sacrifice contracts

If you are defending against a sacrifice contract you must know
what you need for a good score. You have already seen in
chapter 15 how declarer, playing in a sacrifice contract of 4♠
doubled against an opponent's 4♡, must aim at all costs to keep
his penalty below the value of the opponents' game. If opponents
are vulnerable there will be far less difference between −300 and
−500 than there would be between −500 and −800, because
−620 and −650 lie between these numbers. If they are not
vulnerable −500 will compare very unfavourably with −420 or
−450. Of course, if opponents have sacrificed against your game
contract you must aim for a bigger penalty than your game.

```
              ♠ 10 9 6 5
              ♡ 9 5              Game all
              ♢ K Q J 10 8      Dealer East
              ♣ K 6            South  West  North  East
♠ A 4 3          N                                 1♡
♡ K 8 6 2      W   E           1♠     3♡    3♠     4♡
♢ 9 6 2          S             No     No    4♠     Dble
♣ A 5 3                        No     No    No
```

East takes your ♡ 2 lead with the ♡ A and returns the ♡ Q,
South following suit. East has at most five hearts so he doesn't
seem to have bid game on wild distribution, therefore he must
have a better than minimum opening bid. In that case South's
vulnerable overcall must be very weak, and it is quite likely that
at least some East/West pairs will have been allowed to play in
4♡ undisturbed. If 4♡ is due to fail you will get a good score for
even +200, so assume 4♡ makes. You need +800 (three off) to
beat +620, and the most likely source of six tricks must be the
♠ A, two hearts, the ♢ A and ♣ A Q. Therefore overtake the
♡ Q with the ♡ K and switch to the ♣ 3, hoping East has
the ♣ Q, but not the ♣ J, and declarer misguesses.

Quiz
1) For hands a) and b) give your lead as West after each of the
   sequences below:

   a) ♠ Q 10 3   ♡ 7 6 5   ♢ A Q 7 4   ♣ Q 10 8
   b) ♠ Q 9 3 2   ♡ 9   ♢ A Q 7 4 2 ♣ 9 6 2

i)	South	North	ii)	South	North	iii)	South	North
	1NT	3NT		1♡	3♡		1♠	3♠
				4♡			4♠	

```
2)                       ♠ 8 7 5 4
                         ♡ A K Q J
                         ♢ K J 8
                         ♣ K 6         Love all
                                       Dealer North
         ♠ A Q 10 2        N           South  North
         ♡ 9 6           W   E                  1♡
         ♢ A 4 2           S           1NT      2NT
         ♣ Q J 10 9
```

a) Your ♣ Q lead against 2NT is won by dummy's ♣ K, and at trick 2 dummy's ◇ J is led. Plan the defence.

b) Now plan the defence if South had raised North's 2NT game try to 3NT.

3)

```
              ♠ A Q J 10 9 8
              ♡ A
              ◇ 9 8 6                Game all
              ♣ K Q J               Dealer North
 ♠ 6                                 South     North
 ♡ Q J 5                                       1♠
 ◇ A 10 7 4 2                        1NT       2NT
 ♣ A 10 8 4                          3NT
```

Your ◇ 4 lead goes to partner's ◇ J and declarer's ◇ K. He now leads the ♣ 2. Plan the defence.

4)

```
              ♠ Q J 8 2
              ♡ K J
              ◇ A K Q J 10 9        Love all
              ♣ 5                   Dealer North
 ♠ A 6 5                             South     North
 ♡ A 9 5 4                                     1◇
 ◇ 8 7                               1♠        3♠
 ♣ K Q 10 3                          3NT
```

You lead the ♣ K against 3NT. Declarer wins the ♣ A (partner contributing the ♣ 2) and leads the ♠ K, taken by your ♠ A. Plan the defence.

5)

```
              ♠ 9 2
              ♡ K 8 5 4
              ◇ K 8 7               Love all
              ♣ K J 10 4            Dealer South
 ♠ A Q 10 7 5                        South  West   North  East
 ♡ J 9 3                             1♡     1♠     3♡     4♠
 ◇ 9 6 5                             5♡     No     No     No
 ♣ 9 2
```

Your ♣ 9 lead strikes gold as East produces the ♣ A Q and gives you a ruff. What next?

6)

```
              ♠ 6
              ♡ J 10 9 6 3
              ◇ Q J              North/South Game
              ♣ Q 6 4 3 2        Dealer South
  ♠ K 5                          South  West  North  East
  ♡ A Q 5         N              1◇     No    1♡     3♠
  ◇ 10 9 4 3   W     E           3NT    No    No     No
  ♣ K J 10 9       S
```

Your ♠ K lead holds trick 1. Plan the defence.

7)

```
              ♠ K J 10           Love all
              ♡ 9 3              Dealer North
              ◇ Q J 10 5 4       South  West  North  East
              ♣ 9 4 3                         No     No
  ♠ A 2                          3◇     Dble  5◇     6♣
  ♡ K Q 7 2       N              No     No    6◇     No
  ◇ A 6        W     E           No     Dble  No     No
  ♣ K Q 8 5 2      S             No
```

Your ♣ K lead is ruffed and declarer leads the ◇ 3 from his hand. Plan the defence.

8)

```
  ♠ Q 3                          Love all
  ♡ 8 4 3                        Dealer South
  ◇ A K 10 9 6 3                 South  West  North  East
  ♣ K 9                          1♠     No    2◇     No
        N        ♠ 8 7 4         3♠     No    4♠     No
     W     E     ♡ 9 7 5 2       No     No
        S        ◇ 8 5
                 ♣ A 8 6 2
```

Your partner leads the ♣ Q to dummy's ♣ K and your ♣ A. How do you continue:
a) playing rubber bridge?   b) playing duplicate pairs?

Answer to quiz

1) a) i) The ♡ 6. Give nothing away.

ii) The ♡ 5. Passive, but at the same time cutting down declarer's ruffing power in dummy.

iii) Again the ♡ 6. It is not a good idea to lead from a trump holding like ♠ Q 10 3.

   b) i) The ♢ 4. This time you have a five-card suit. It might cost a trick, but the potential gain is greater.

   ii) The ♣ 6. The ♠ 2 is a possible alternative which would be more attractive playing teams. A singleton trump lead is *not* recommended.

   iii) The ♡ 9. You don't desperately want a ruff with this trump holding, but you may make your ♠ Q anyway.

2) a) Declarer plainly has the ♣ A and very likely the ♢ Q. With the ♠ K he would surely have raised 2NT to 3NT, so switch to the ♠ 2 and collect your five tricks.

   b) This time declarer must have the ♠ K as well, so exit passively with a club.

3) Declarer's failure to attack the spade suit immediately marks him with the ♠ K. He must also have either the ♡ K, or the ♢ Q, but not both. You don't know which of the hands below he has, but you must be aware that the rest of the field will be in 4♠, played by North.

   i) ♠ K 3 2   ♡ 9 7 4 2   ♢ K Q 3   ♣ 9 7 3
   ii) ♠ K 3 2   ♡ K 9 4 2   ♢ K 5 3   ♣ 9 7 3

If he has i) those in 4♠ will make ten tricks. Since you cannot now prevent ten tricks in 3NT you will score badly whatever you do!

   If he has ii) he will either make 4♠ or go one off, depending on the lead. You also can beat 3NT by taking your ♣ A and laying down the ♢ A.

   You must plainly cater for ii) and play the ♢ A.

4) North is insane! Everybody else will rebid 4♠, and they will be unlikely to lose more than the ♠ A and one heart. Therefore cash your ♣ K and ♡ A, confident that −430 will give you a good score. Underleading your ♡ A may defeat the contract spectacularly if East has the ♡ Q and declarer misguesses, but that is not likely. If you try it and lose 3 spades, the ♡ K, 6 diamonds and the ♣ A you will find that −460 will be a complete bottom! Besides, most defenders will similarly cash the ♡ A against 4♠, scoring −450 *whoever* has the ♡ Q!

5) Cash the ♠ A! Not everybody will have overcalled with your hand at *Love all* and most Souths will be in 4♡ going one off, or perhaps even making if West doesn't find the club lead. Two off will undoubtedly be worth an excellent score. If you greedily underlead your ♠ A in the hope that partner's fourth club will promote your ♡ J, or sit back thinking your ♠ A cannot run away, you will undo all your good work so far. Declarer probably has something like:

   ♠ K 4   ♡ A Q 10 7 6 2   ◇ A Q   ♣ 8 7 3

6) This looks promising, but before continuing with a second spade, pause for thought! Suppose declarer has:

   ♠ A 8 3   ♡ K 2   ◇ A K 8 7 6 5   ♣ A 5

   He has eight top tricks and you will inevitably have to give him a ninth in the endgame. The spectacular, but safe, continuation is the ♣ K, removing the only entry to his hand before he can unblock the ◇ Q J. If he has a third club he might duck your ♣ K, but at least you tried!

   Note that even at pairs you *must* aim to beat this contract. It is possible that declarer's hand may be weaker than that, but if partner's pre-empt has pushed North/South too high you should score well anyway.

7) Since declarer has no clubs and only six diamonds, he has seven major suit cards. Presumably he has either four spades and three hearts, or vice versa. Not all Souths will have pre-empted with a miserable six-card suit, so you must concentrate on scoring more than the 920 you would have achieved for making 6♣. You can safely assume that East has the ♡ A for his 6♣ bid. If declarer has the ♠ Q you cannot make more than four tricks (the ♠ A, 2 hearts and the ◇ A). The resulting 500 will beat game (420 or 480) but not a slam. How about if East has the ♠ Q? You have a chance of achieving the magic 1100 by rising with your ◇ A and switching to the ♠ 2! If declarer misguesses, East will win the ♠ Q and you should get a ruff, using his ♡ A as an entry. It can't hurt to try, as your tricks can hardly run away!

8) a) However unlikely it may seem, you must look for an opportunity to beat 4♠. It is just possible that declarer has:

♠ A K J 10 9 2　　♡ K J　　◇ Q J 2　　♣ 7 3

In that case you must switch to a heart.

b) While declarer may have the hand above, it is far more likely that he has the ♡ A, for example:

♠ A K J 10 9 2　　♡ A 6　　◇ Q J 2　　♣ 7 3

In that case a heart return will allow him to draw trumps and claim twelve tricks. Therefore give up on the slight chance of beating the contract and return a club.

17. Signals and Discards

When your partner leads a low card in a suit you normally attempt to win the trick or, failing that, to force out as high a card as possible from declarer's hand, hopefully promoting a winner in your hand or partner's. The principle of not giving declarer a cheap trick leads to the 'third hand plays high' rule. If dummy has played a card you cannot beat, or partner has led an honour, you must contribute a card with no thought of winning the trick. You should choose your card carefully as your *Signal* will give partner a message. Traditionally an *unnecessarily* high card encourages partner to persevere with the suit, while a small card denies interest. Of course it is rewarding to communicate smoothly with your partner in this way, but inexperienced players tend to signal too much. This results in either giving information that is more useful to declarer than partner, or even worse, using a card to signal that could have had a trick-taking role later in the hand. The futility of this is usually magnified by the fact that most of what you signal, *partner can work out for himself*. To illustrate this claim, consider the following typical example.

On lead against 4♠ you lead the ♡ 2 from ♡ K 10 4 2. Dummy, producing ♡ A 8 3 and no particular surprises, rises with the ♡ A and leads a trump to your ♠ A. Do you really need partner to signal that he has the ♡ Q? *If declarer had it he would surely have played low from dummy at trick 1!*

Of course there are occasions when an 'encouraging' signal is helpful, but they are less common than you might imagine. If you are satisfied with your signalling system by all means turn to the next chapter, but if you are prepared to take the trouble to count declarer's shape you should carefully consider the merits of *Length Signals*. They are *not* a totally new concept but an extension of what you probably already play in certain well-defined circumstances. For instance:

i) Defending against a suit contract you start a *Peter* with a small doubleton by playing the higher card if partner leads an honour or dummy wins partner's lead. This helps partner to judge whether you can ruff the third round of the suit.

ii) If declarer is trying to establish dummy's suit with few entries, you play *High Low* to show an even number of cards in the suit. This might help partner to take his ace at the right moment to isolate declarer from dummy's winners.

iii) If you have exactly three trumps and are void in a side suit you make the rare, but invaluable, *Trump Peter*.

i) and ii) are normal length signals, playing high/low to show an even number. The principle is the same in iii) except the signal is reversed (high/low showing an *odd* number of trumps).

If you and your partner agree to play *Length Signals* you give up 'encouraging' and 'discouraging' signals in favour of always signalling 'high/low' with an even number of cards in the suit led, *unless you can judge it will help declarer more than partner*. This last qualification cannot be stressed too much, as if you gain the reputation of automatically signalling length declarer will rarely guess wrongly when faced with a choice between a taking a finesse or playing for a missing high card to drop.

Of course, your signals should be systematic. Suppose partner leads the ♡ K and you have ♡ 8 6 4 3. Play the ♡ 6, your *second highest*, and complete your signal next time with your original fourth highest ♡ 3. The reason for this is that the second highest from four usually gives an immediate impression of being unnecessarily high, while at the same time it is a card you can usually afford. With an odd number of cards in the suit start with the lowest and work up. As with any signalling system, if there is any danger that the systemic signal could cost a trick you must improvise. Suppose partner leads the ♢ A, dummy produces the ♢ 8 4 2, and you have the ♢ J 10 7 5. The ♢ 10 will cost a trick if declarer has ♢ Q 9 3, so play the ♢ 7.

Apart from being indispensible in helping partner count shape, length signals are very useful when you must judge how many tricks in a suit you can cash before declarer ruffs. Consider this example:

```
              ♠ K J 4
              ♡ 8 5 3
              ♢ A K Q J        East/West Game
              ♣ Q J 8          Dealer South
 ♠ 9 5 2       ┌─────┐         South    North
 ♡ K Q J 10    │  N  │         3♠       4♠
 ♢ 8 3 2       │W   E│
 ♣ A 7 4       │  S  │
              └─────┘
```

You lead the ♡ K, partner signals with the ♡ 7, and declarer follows with the ♡ 4. Partner, with an even number of hearts, clearly has the ♡ A and a four-card suit because:

 i) Declarer should not open 3♠ with four hearts.
 ii) Declarer would have no reason to duck the ♡ A.

Plainly as soon as declarer seizes the lead he will rattle off seven spade tricks and four diamonds, therefore you must cash exactly one more heart before switching to the ♣ A followed by the ♣ 7. Continue with the ♡ Q at trick 2, indicating that you know what to do and want to retain the lead.

The McKenny Signal

Whatever your agreed system of leads and signals there are plainly times when partner has a desperate need for information about your preference between the *other* suits. In these cases it is your responsibility to use your small, or intermediate, cards in the suit led to tell him what switch you want. This is called a *McKenny* signal, and the principle is as follows:

If you ignore the suit led there are three other suits. Usually the return of one of them is clearly pointless (often the trump suit), leaving just two. An unnecessarily high card asks for the higher ranking of these two suits, while a small card requests the lower ranking suit. The most common use is indicating a switch when giving partner a ruff. Suppose he leads the ♣ 2 against 4♡, an obvious singleton on the bidding. Dummy has ♣ K Q J and you have ♣ A 9 7 5 4 3. Your ambition is to give him two ruffs, and to that effect you must indicate what switch you want at trick 3. Take your ♣ A and return the ♣ 9 if you have the ♠ A (the higher ranking suit) or the ♣ 3 if you have the ◇ A (the lower ranking suit).

Sometimes the McKenny principle can be extended to include the trump suit!

```
                  ♠ K Q 3
                  ♡ Q 4 3 2
                  ◇ K 3 2              Love all
                  ♣ K Q 4             Dealer South
    ♠ A 6 2                           South    North
    ♡ 9 5              N              1♡       2♣
    ◇ Q J 10 9 8    W     E           2♡       4♡
    ♣ 8 3 2            S
```

Your ◇ Q wins trick 1, partner contributing the ◇ 4. You cannot read any length meaning into this as he would have played the ◇ 4 from ◇ A 4 doubleton as well as from ◇ A 6 4. So it is possible that his doubleton ace will win trick 2 and he will be looking for a quick re-entry into your hand. Continue with the ◇ J, a McKenny signal demanding a spade switch. Such a switch is necessary as declarer holds:

♠ J 8 7   ♡ A K J 10 8   ◇ 7 6 4   ♣ A 6

If your entry had been the ♣ A your continuation at trick 2 would have been the ◇ 8. Even if your entry had been the ♡ A there would have been a reasonable chance of partner reading the ♡ 10 as a demand for a trump. It would have been very necessary if South had held:

♠ A 7 5   ♡ K J 10 8 7   ◇ 7 6 5   ♣ A 6

The ◇ 10 certainly would deny the ♠ A as the ◇ J continuation would then have been clearcut, but West might have been in some difficulty if his original diamond holding had been ◇ Q J 10 6. In practice this is rarely a problem as the sight of dummy usually immediately rules out one of the side suits.

Discards

There is nothing more difficult in bridge than discarding as declarer reels off his long suit, and the consequences of incorrect discarding are magnified at duplicate pairs when every overtrick counts!

As with signalling systems, you can persevere with the idea that a high card encourages, or agree methods based on the McKenny principle when you can use a discard in one suit to indicate interest in another, or abandon all that in favour of signalling length. It is comparatively easy to combine methods because it is usually possible to show where your values lie with just one discard. Therefore I recommend that you use only the first discard to encourage or discourage, thereafter showing length in the suit discarded. For example, if declarer runs a seven-card diamond suit and partner follows to two rounds, and then discards the ♠ 2, ♠ 7, ♣ 3, ♠ 4 and ♣ 5, his first discard shows no interest in spades, and he subsequently shows he started with an even number of spades and an odd number of clubs. You should not find it too difficult to work out the heart position!

Finally, a word of warning! As with signalling, you must work out whether a true length count will help partner or declarer. Often it is clear that declarer has alternative options in playing a suit, and is trying to get a count. *Only tell partner what he needs to know!*

Quiz
1) ♠ 9 6 4
   ♡ K 7 3
   ◇ A K J 10
   ♣ K 6 5

	Game all
	Dealer South
♠ 2	South North
♡ J 10 9 8	2NT 6NT
◇ 9 5 4 3	
♣ J 10 9 8	

Your partner leads the ♠ Q, won by declarer's ♠ A. He now

cashes four rounds of diamonds, East following to the first two
and then discarding the ♠ 7 and ♡ 2. At trick 6 he leads the ♠ 6
from dummy. What do you discard?

2)   ♠ 8 4
                       ♡ 9 8 6 5 3
                       ◇ K Q J   *Love all*
                       ♣ K 6 4   Dealer South
    ♠ A K Q J 7   ┌─────────┐   South West   North East
    ♡ 7 2   │   N   │   1♡   1♠   3♡   4♠
    ◇ 6 4   │ W   E │   5◇   No   5♡   No
    ♣ Q J 10 3   │   S   │   No   No
                   └─────────┘

You lead the ♠ A against 5♡. What is your defence if:
  i) partner follows with the ♠ 2 and declarer with the ♠ 6.
  ii) partner follows with the ♠ 6 and declarer with the ♠ 2.

3)   ♠ 8 3
                       ♡ 10 8 3
                       ◇ K J 4 3   *Love all*
                       ♣ A 10 9 2   Dealer South
    ♠ 9 6   ┌─────────┐   South   North
    ♡ 9 6 4   │   N   │   1♠   1NT
    ◇ A 8 5 2   │ W   E │   3♡   3NT
    ♣ K Q J 8   │   S   │   4♠
                   └─────────┘

Your ♣ K loses to dummy's ♣ A, declarer leads the ♠ 3 to
his ♠ Q, and continues with the ◇ 7. Plan the defence if:
  i) partner's card to trick 1 was the ♣ 6.
  ii) partner's card in trick 1 was the ♣ 3.

4) ♠ 9 7 5 3
    ♡ 8
    ◇ K J 10 2   *East/West Game*
    ♣ K J 10 2   Dealer East
    ┌─────────┐   ♠ A K J 10 8 2   South West   North East
    │   N   │   ♡ 4   1♠
    │ W   E │   ◇ A Q 3   4♡   No   No   No
    │   S   │   ♣ 6 4 3
    └─────────┘

Partner leads the ♠ Q. Plan the defence.

5) ♠ Q J 5
    ♡ Q J 2
    ◇ 10 8 5   *East/West Game*
    ♣ A K Q J   Dealer South

♠ A K 4   South   West   North   East
♡ A K 8 7 5   N   5◇   Dble   No   No
◇ A   W   E   No
♣ 8 6 3 2   S

On your ♠ A lead partner follows with the ♠ 7 and declarer
with the ♠ 10. What next?

6) ♠ 10 5 3 2
    ♡ A K
    ◇ 8 4 3   *Game all*
    ♣ A Q J 2   Dealer South

          N   ♠ K 7 4   South   North
    W   E   ♡ Q 6 3 2   1♠   2♣
          S   ◇ K 9 2   2♠   4♠
                      ♣ K 10 5

West leads the ◇ Q. Declarer takes his ◇ A and leads the
♣ 4 to dummy's ♣ Q, West following suit with the ♣ 8. Plan
the defence.

7) ♠ J 6
    ♡ A 8
    ◇ K Q J 10 9 6   *Game all*
    ♣ 9 7 4   Dealer South

♠ 9 3   N   South   North
♡ J 7 3   W   E 1NT *   3NT
◇ A 5 2   S
♣ A 10 8 6 2   *1NT shows 12-14 HCP.

As West you lead the ♣ 6 to partner's ♣ J and declarer's
♣ K. Declarer continues with the ◇ 7. Plan the defence.

Answers to quiz

1) Since partner has the ♠ Q J, declarer must have every other
   missing high card for his 2NT. That gives him twelve tricks (2
   spades, 3 hearts, 4 diamonds and 3 clubs). You must now
   discard correctly to prevent the overtrick. The key is in

partner's ♡ 2 discard, showing an odd number (presumably three). Therefore declarer also has three hearts and you can safely discard a heart.

2) i) Partner has an odd number of spades, presumably five in view of his aggressive bidding on minimal values. Switch to the ♣ Q and try to take two club tricks before dummy's clubs disappear on declarer's five-card diamond suit.

ii) Partner has only four spades, so cash the ♠ K before switching to the ♣ Q. Note that if you fail to cash your ♠ K *partner will assume there isn't another spade to cash!* Then if your ♣ Q is covered by dummy's ♣ K and East's ♣ A he will try to cash a second club. If declarer ruffs that, draws trumps, and discards dummy's spades on his diamonds you will be to blame!

3) South's bidding marks him with 6 spades and 4 hearts. With 7 spades he might have gone straight to 4♠ and with 5 hearts he would have continued with 4♡ over 3NT. The vital question is: 'What is his minor suit shape?'

i) Partner is showing an even number of clubs, plainly four. Therefore South has one club and 2 diamonds. Play a low diamond and hope he misguesses.

ii) Partner is showing an odd number of clubs. This time declarer has one diamond and two clubs so rise with the ♢ A and continue clubs.

4) This might be the last chance to ensure a diamond switch, so leave him on lead, contributing the ♠ J as a McKenny signal to ask for a switch to the higher ranking of the two minor suits.

5) You hadn't expected a great deal of difficulty in beating 5♢, but the sight of dummy's club suit makes it plain that you must cash the right major suit winner at trick two! East clearly has an even number of spades, but has he four or six? The key lies in correctly interpreting his ♠ 7! With ♠ 9 8 7 6 3 2 he would have played the ♠ 8, his *second highest*, so it is safe to continue with the ♠ K. Declarer seems to have:

♠ 10 8 2   ♡ —   ♢ K Q J 9 7 6 4 3 2   ♣ 7

6) West's high club promises an even number of cards in the suit, plainly four as if declarer had four clubs he would have no reason to delay drawing trumps. Therefore declarer is hoping to quickly discard a losing diamond on dummy's third club if the finesse is right. It seems right to take your ♣ K (before it runs away) and cash whatever you can in diamonds, but consider the effect of ducking! Admittedly declarer could score an outright top by drawing trumps with the aid of a finesse and ruffing out your ♣ K, although there isn't much danger of that! He will be reassured that the club finesse is working, and anxious to repeat it in the search for overtricks! Since he has no quick entries to his hand outside the trump suit he will have two choices. If he successfully takes a trump finesse and then finesses the ♣ J you can still cash your diamonds. But if he decides to 'ensure' an overtrick by playing a spade to his ♠ A to repeat the club finesse, your subterfuge will have earned you a deserved, and spectacular, top.

The moral here is that the old adage of refusing a finesse that is likely to be repeated is just as relevant at duplicate pairs. Even if declarer suspects you of deception, he can hardly risk a bottom by refusing a second club finesse when he has every reason to believe that the rest of the room will successfully take it!

7) The question is, 'Does partner have the ♣ Q or should you be looking for his entry so he can lead clubs through declarer?' You will find out by ducking trick 2 to dummy's ◇ K. If he does have the ♣ Q he will know from your fourth-highest lead that declarer has no club higher than the ♣ 6 left, so he should convey the good news to you by discarding the ♣ Q on the ◇ Q at trick 3, leaving your club suit high.

18. Modern Lead Systems

. Standard leads

As with signals and discards, there are a number of methods in common use, each with its own band of devoted followers. This time I don't intend to suggest abandoning traditional methods of leading 'fourth highest' and 'top of a sequence', but merely to clarify them, and improve on them. Firstly, it is worth spending a little time explaining standard leads.

If you choose to lead from a suit with at least four cards it is normally correct to lead a low card (fourth best for information purposes). Leading from a holding like ♠ K J 7 4 2 against no trumps is an *Attacking* lead, potentially lucrative if partner has an honour but likely to cost a trick if he has only small cards in the suit. As you have already seen, you are more inclined to be passive when defending at pairs, but it is still normal practice to lead from a good five-card suit against a no-trump contract if you have outside entries. If partner has ♠ Q 8 he will rise with the ♠ Q (third hand plays high), return the suit if declarer ducks, and you might make four tricks if the missing spades are split 3-3. If, as declarer, you were attacking a suit of ♠ K J 7 4 2 opposite ♠ Q 8 you would lead towards the ♠ Q first to avoid blocking the suit. The principle is the same in defence, even if you cannot see partner's holding.

It is far better to lead from a solid suit, e.g., ♠ K Q J 3 2, because you combine all the attacking possibilities of establishing spot card winners with a far greater degree of safety. You lead the ♠ K (top of a sequence) *because this time you don't expect to need help from partner in establishing your suit.* By the time your ♠ K Q J have been played, only the enemy ♠ A offering any resistance, it is likely that you will be the only player with spades left, so your lowly ♠ 3 2 will have become winners. However if you chose to lead from this holding against a no-trump contract *after an opponent had bid spades* (more likely at rubber bridge than at pairs) it is clear that your honours would not clear all the enemy spades, therefore you would need help from partner (perhaps the ♠ 10) so it would be correct to lead the ♠ 3.

Most tables of standard leads are defective because they fail to take account of clues from the bidding, and the number of outside entries you have. For example, if South's 1NT is raised to 3NT and you have no outside entry to maintain communication with partner, lead the ♠ 10 from ♠ A K 10 9 8. If you also miraculously have the two minor suit aces you cannot expect partner to have anything, so make the lead that gives you the best chance of establishing the suit for only one loser, the ♠ A. If declarer has ♠ Q 3 and dummy has ♠ J 7 6 2, the ♠ 10 lead gives him two guards. On a really lucky day you might even find declarer with ♠ Q 3 and dummy with ♠ J 7. (You did double, didn't you?)

To decide between the rival merits of an honour lead and fourth highest you should analyse your motives for leading the suit. If you then decide that you require partner to have an honour card to succeed, lead your fourth highest. On the other hand, if you have a reasonable chance of achieving your objective without his help, lead an honour rather than risk giving away a cheap trick. Here are some examples:

Leading from ♠ K Q 5 4 2 against a suit contract your objective must be to establish just one winner, because somebody will be ruffing the third round (hopefully partner). Therefore lead the ♠ K. On the other hand, leading from the same holding against a no-trump contract you are aiming to establish several winners and need partner to hold something like ♠ J 3, so lead the ♠ 4. You may even be lucky if dummy holds ♠ J 9 8 and partner has just ♠ 10 3 because declarer is likely to misguess!

Leading from ♠ K Q 10 8 4 it is worth leading the ♠ K even against no trumps, because declarer or dummy might have a holding like ♠ J 7. Alternatively if declarer has the ♠ A J 7 and ducks you can switch suit, waiting for partner to pierce declarer's remaining ♠ A J holding later. Note that partner will deduce from your ♠ K that you have the ♠ Q *and at least the* ♠ *10*, so he will sacrifice his ♠ J under your ♠ K to encourage you to continue the suit if that is the right defence.

Finally a subject that is too often ignored. Suppose your partner's ♠ 2 lead against 3NT is taken by your ♠ A, and you decide to return the suit. If you started with three spades it is correct to return your *next highest*. On the other hand if you started with four (or more) return your original *fourth highest*.

Thus return the ♠ 8 from ♠ A 8 4, or the ♠ 3 from ♠ A 8 4 3.
Occasionally it might be correct to deviate from this rule if you
must hold the lead in order to pin an honour in declarer's hand,
e.g. you must return the ♠ 10 from ♠ A J 10 4 in case declarer
has the ♠ Q 7 5 2.

The following example demonstrates the need for precision in
these circumstances:

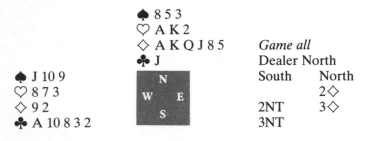

```
              ♠ 8 5 3
              ♡ A K 2
              ◇ A K Q J 8 5     Game all
              ♣ J               Dealer North
♠ J 10 9        N               South      North
♡ 8 7 3       W   E                        2◇
◇ 9 2           S               2NT        3◇
♣ A 10 8 3 2                    3NT
```

Your ♣ 3 lead is won by partner's ♣ K. If he returns the ♣ 7 to
declarer's ♣ 9 and your ♣ 10 you can tell that the ♣ 7 could not
be fourth highest, therefore declarer still has the guarded ♣ Q
and you must try to find partner's entry so he can pierce declarer's remaining club holding. On the other hand if he returned
the ♣ 4 either he started with a doubleton (in which case he
could tell declarer had at least five clubs and might have switched
suits) or with four, in which case your club winners are ripe for
picking.

Second highest leads from bad suits

Consider your dilemma here if partner leads the ♠ 5 and you
have to decide what to return after taking your ♠ A.

```
♠ 9 4
♡ Q 10 6
◇ A K Q J 10 9        Game all
♣ A K                 Dealer North
  N        ♠ A Q 3    South      North
W   E      ♡ K J 9 8                        2◇
  S        ◇ 8 3      2NT        3◇
           ♣ Q J 9 4  3NT
```

The critical missing cards are the ♠ K J and the ♡ A. On the information available to you the percentage play is undoubtedly to return the ♠ Q, hoping that partner has led from ♠ K 9 7 5 2. Sometimes partner may have nothing more exciting than ♠ 10 7 6 5 2, giving declarer ♠ K J 9 and an easy path to ten tricks. Worse still, if declarer has these cards partner has the ♡ A (remember South's 2NT negative response), so a heart switch at trick two would have enabled you to take the first five tricks.

For this reason strong tournament players only lead fourth highest from suits with a picture card (jack or higher). Holding four or more small cards it is best to lead the second highest, a card which usually has little trick-taking potential but can be easily read as denying a high card. This principle is not totally new to you as you probably already lead the ♠ 7 from ♠ 9 7 3 (*Mud*-Middle, Up, Down) but the ♠ 3 from ♠ K 7 3 or ♠ J 7 3. If it is sensible to distinguish between holdings with an honour and those without when you have three cards in the suit, it is surely just as useful to do the same if you have a longer holding.

On seeing a ♠ 7 lead you may not initially be able to tell whether partner has only three, or more, but all will be revealed on the next round. With an initial three-card holding he follows up with the highest (MUD), while with an initial holding of four or more cards he continues with his original fourth best.

Now let us return to the original example. Playing 'second highest from bad suits', you couldn't have distinguished between ♠ K 9 7 5 2 and ♠ J 9 7 5 2. However with ♠ 10 7 6 5 2 he would have led the ♠ 7, marking declarer with the ♠ K J and making it easy for you to find the lethal heart switch.

Strong ten leads

Now consider this very similar problem.

♠ 9 4
♡ Q 10 6
◇ A K Q J 10 9
♣ A K

			Game all	
			Dealer North	
N		♠ A 5 3	South	North
W **E**		♡ K J 9 8		2◇
		◇ 8 3	2NT	3◇
S		♣ Q J 9 4	3NT	

This time partner leads the ♠ J, again taken by your ♠ A. If he has led from ♠ K J 10 7 2 a spade return will ensure the first five tricks, but if he has only ♠ J 10 9 7 2 declarer has the ♠ K Q, marking partner with the ♡ A.

The modern way of avoiding this embarrassing dilemma is to lead a jack *only if you have no higher honour*. With ♠ K J 10 7 2 lead the ♠ 10 which, unless it is a singleton or doubleton, guarantees a touching honour (either the ♠ J or ♠ 9), and at least one card higher than the jack. Thus in our example the ♠ J lead would conclusively point to a heart switch. On the other hand if he had led the ♠ 10 you know the touching honour is the ♠ J as the ♠ 9 is visible in dummy, and since he would still have led the ♠ Q from a sequence headed by ♠ Q J 10, he must also have the ♠ K.

A table of leads

Having earlier urged caution on standard lead tables, I will now invite caustic comments by giving you one to demonstrate the effect of 'second highest' and 'strong ten' leads.

Holding	Lead	Comment
K Q J 10 2	K	No change
Q J 10 7 2	Q	No change
J 10 9 7 2	J	The jack denies a higher honour
A J 10 7 2	10	
K J 10 7 2	10	
A 10 9 7 2	10	
Q 10 9 7 2	10	
10 9 8 7 2	9	Second highest from a suit without an honour. Followed by the 7 (fourth best)
10 9 8	9	Followed by the 10
9 7 5 4	7	Followed by the 4
9 7 5	7	Followed by the 9

Quiz

1) Your partner leads a heart against 3NT. Dummy has ♡ Q 9 3 and you have ♡ A 6. Work out as much as you can about partner's heart holding if his lead was each of the following cards.

a) ♡ 2   b) ♡ 4   c) ♡ 8   d) ♡ 10   e) ♡ J

2) ♠ 8 7 5 2
   ♡ 8 6
   ♦ 9 5 3   *Game all*
   ♣ A K Q J   Dealer West

	♠ K 9 4 3	South	West	North	East
N	♡ A Q 2		2♡	No	3♡
W E	♦ 7 6 4 2	3♠	No	4♠	No
S	♣ 7 2	No	No		

Having opened a weak 2♡, West leads the ♡ 10. Plan the defence.

3) ♠ K J 3
   ♡ Q 7 3
   ♦ A K Q J   *North/South Game*
   ♣ K 6 3   Dealer North

	♠ A Q 10 4 2	South	West	North	East
N	♡ 8 2			1♦	1♠
W E	♦ 9 6 3 2	4♡	4♠	5♡	No
S	♣ 9 5	No	No		

West leads the ♠ 6 against 5♡ and you take dummy's ♠ J with your ♠ Q, declarer following with the ♠ 9. Plan the defence.

4) ♠ A Q 6 2
   ♡ K 9
   ♦ 9 7 5 2   *Love all*
   ♣ A Q J   Dealer South

	♠ 8 5 3	South	North
N	♡ 6 3 2	1NT	2♣
W E	♦ A 4 3	2♦	3NT
S	♣ 10 9 3 2		

West leads the ♡ 10, won by dummy's ♡ K. Declarer then calls for dummy's ♦ 2. Plan the defence.

5) ♠ 3
♥ K J 6 2   *Love all*
♦ A K J 6   Dealer South
♣ K 9 4 2

	South	North
♠ A 6 2	1NT	2♣
♥ Q 10 5 3	2♠	3NT
♦ Q 7 3 2		
♣ J 10	1NT shows 12–14 HCP	

West leads the ♠ J. How do you plan to defend?

Answers to quiz

1) a) The ♥ 2 is fourth best from exactly four. Partner has the
♥ J, or ♥ K, or both.
   b) The ♥ 4 is fourth best from four or five. As above, partner
has the ♥ J or ♥ K or both.
   c) The ♥ 8 is second best from ♥ 10 8 x or ♥ 10 8 x x (x).
From ♥ K J 10 8 (x) he would have led the ♥ 10.
   d) The ♥ 10 is from ♥ K J 10 x (x). Without the ♥ K he
would have led the ♥ J.
   e) The ♥ J is from ♥ J 10 8 (x). Without the ♥ 8 he would
have led his fourth highest.

2) Your object here must be to take your heart and diamond
tricks before declarer can draw trumps and discard losers on
dummy's clubs. You have some time on your side because
dummy does not have sufficient entries to pick up your
♠ K, but if declarer has a diamond holding of ♦ A Q 10 or
♦ A J 10 you will have to lead diamonds through him twice in
order to pick up your dues. Partner's ♥ 10 guarantees the
♥ K, so you can see that the heart suit provides the necessary
entries. If you take trick 1 with the ♥ A partner will not know
who has the ♥ Q and will not underlead his ♥ K. Therefore
win the ♥ Q and switch to the ♦ 6.

3) You must plainly take your winners before you are sub-
   merged by declarer's red cards. Perhaps you think West
   should have four spades for his aggressive 4♠, however a
   detailed inspection of the spot cards tells a different story!
   The missing spades are ♠ 8 7 5, but West would have led the
   ♠ 7 from ♠ 8 7 6 5. Therefore you can safely cash a second
   spade before switching to the ♣ 9.

4) West has led the ♡ 10 from ♡ A J 10 x x, (remember South's
   2♢ response to Stayman denied a four-card major), so rise
   with the ♢ A and fire back a heart.

5) Defending this hand is an open book, if you are prepared to
   count points! West's ♠ J denies a higher honour, therefore
   South has ♠ K Q x x. He cannot have 12 HCP without the
   ♡ A and ♣ A; if he also had the ♣ Q he would have 15 HCP
   so West must have that card. With so few entries to West's
   hand you are most unlikely to establish his spades, therefore
   you must concentrate on passive defence. You should start by
   withholding your ♠ A on trick 1, allowing declarer to make
   his ♠ Q but denying him a second trick in the suit. When you
   regain the lead, probably with one of your red queens, you
   should abandon spades and aim to exit as passively as
   possible.

19. Creating Tops and Bottoms

Estimating your percentage

Many pairs are content to enjoy their evening without keeping tally of their progress; others like to estimate their score as they go along. They give themselves an estimated score out of ten for each hand, and record it on their personal scorecard. Late in the evening when you can see the results already achieved at other tables this is easy, but early on you have only your judgement to go on. Sometimes you will have to accept a poor score through no fault of your own. Let us imagine how your thought processes may go:

i) You open 1NT with 13 points, and partner passes with balanced 9. The defence is passive and accurate, holding you to 7 tricks. You reluctantly concede to yourself that although you bid to the obvious contract and played it correctly, quite a few declarers will be presented with an overtrick in the same contract.

Estimated score: 3 out of 10

ii) Your opening 1NT (13 points) is doubled by your left-hand opponent with a very poor 15 HCP. He is lucky enough to find his partner with 11 HCP but they slip a trick in defence and you escape for −300. Yes, they can make game, but unfortunately at many tables your 1NT bid will be passed out.

Estimated score: 3 out of 10

iii) You bravely protect with a vulnerable 2♠ over your opponents' known heart fit. Opener carries on to 3♡-1, but you could have made 2♠. You can be optimistic about this because your risky 2♠ may not be generally repeated, and if it is your partner may carry on to a doomed 3♠ over 3♡.

Estimated score: 8 out of 10

iv) You play in 4♡, having used Stayman 2♣ to unearth a 4-4 heart fit after partner's 1NT opening. There is nothing in the play and you make 11 tricks, but 3NT + 2 is also cold on a lucky lie of the cards. Your Stayman bid was correct, but with 3-4-4-2 shape some of the field will have hacked 3NT.

Estimated score: 4 out of 10

v) Opponents bid to a pushy, but reasonable 4♠ with only 24 points. Missing the queen and four small trumps declarer misguesses a two-way finesse, going one down. Some pairs will not bid game, and others will guess the ♠ Q correctly.

Estimated score: 8 out of 10

vi) You daringly sacrifice in 4♠ over a vulnerable 4♡, opponents bid on to 5♡ (which would have gone one off) but partner continues to 5♠ (−500). Again you could have done better, but you judge that most pairs will be conceding −620 to 4♡.

Estimated score: 7 out of 10

vii) Your opponents bid and make an excellent 6♣ with only 30 HCP and a 4-4 trump fit. You gloomily reflect that the vast majority of the field will be in 3NT, and if anybody tries 6NT they have at most 11 tricks.

Estimated score: 1 out of 10

Suppose 20 boards have been played and you estimate your score at 118 out of 200. This is equivalent to 59%, or slightly less than two tops above average. You would generally require something over 60% to win a 24 board movement with a small field (perhaps a 12 table Mitchell) so you seem to be heading for second place. Provided you trust your judgement you might now try to create a couple of abnormal results, hoping they bring you tops. Of course, they are just as likely to bring you bottoms, but you might decide that you will gladly swap your boring second place for a chance of winning. Nevertheless, a word of warning! Sometimes 59% will win or you have done better than you think, and your anti-percentage attempts to create tops will cost you the event! There is nothing more frustrating, and damaging to partnership morale, than to finish with a couple of self-inflicted bottoms only to find that two averages would have sufficed. Playing for tops requires nerve, and a stoic temperament if it misfires!

Perhaps a more realistic time to look for controlled opportunities to create tops is if you are playing to qualify for a final and need to be in the top half. If your score on the first 12 boards was only 43% you don't have too much to lose! However, *don't* try it on every board. Some situations are potentially more promising than others, and you must learn to recognise them.

Playing for tops in the bidding

So the time has come with six boards to play when you decide to shoot for tops. To most players this means wild overbidding, but rest assured that if you leap to 6NT with 16 balanced HCP opposite partner's 1NT opening the odds are heavily that you will collect a richly deserved bottom! However desperate you are, to do anything wild is unnecessary because duplicate pairs is full of situations where the whole room will be taking the 55% chance rather than the 45% chance. If you deliberately take the marginally anti-percentage line you may be successful, and will undoubtedly score well if it works. With such opportunities available, why aim at 10% shots?

Let us now examine the sort of chances you may have to create a swing.

At *Love all* partner opens 1NT. Each of these hands gives you an opportunity:

a) ♠ K J 3   ♡ Q 6 4   ◇ Q 5 4 2   ♣ A 5 2
b) ♠ A K Q J 6 3 ♡ 7 5   ◇ A K 4   ♣ 8 3
c) ♠ 9 5   ♡ A 7 6 5 4 2 ◇ 8 7   ♣ 10 4 3

With a) try passing! Game is unlikely to be gold-plated, and you may be the only pair of your polarity to get a plus score if the cards lie unkindly for you. Deliberately *underbidding* is just as likely to achieve an abnormal result as overbidding.

With b) try 3NT! Perhaps 11 tricks are available in all contracts. Alternatively try 6NT (leaving partner as declarer with his tenaces protected). He might be given it on the opening lead! One thing is certain. If you want to create an abnormal result, don't aim for scientific bidding which will tell your opponents what to lead!

With c) try passing! Perhaps you will go two off with 2♡ cold, but still get a top if everybody else's 2♡ sign off (directly or via a transfer sequence) makes it easy for opponents to protect with 2♠ and score 140.

Another common opportunity to gain a top is to make a slightly unsound penalty double, particularly if you sense the possibility of +200 from vulnerable opponents on a part-score hand.

Psyches

A psyche is very likely to create an abnormal result, but pick your opportunities carefully.

i) If you psyche, make sure your hand really is poor. The purpose of psyching is to create confusion, a reasonable ambition if your opponents have the balance of power but patently absurd if you have the majority of high cards. Psyching with 10 HCP is truly pointless.

ii) Watch the vulnerability. At *Green* vulnerability, not only is your psyche likely to be cheaper, but opponents are less likely to double you as they will be worried that the resulting penalty will be insufficient to compensate them for a missed game.

iii) Your best opportunity to psyche is in third position, since as your partner has already passed there is no chance of sabotaging his rock-crusher.

iv) If you choose to psyche, don't bid a suit in which you hold a singleton or void. Not only is there too great a possibility that partner will support you violently, but also if left to their own devices opponents may find their fit, and fail because of the bad trump break.

v) If you choose to psyche with a suit or no trumps, it can pay to have a long side suit to run to if the going gets sticky! If partner has passed, try overcalling 1♡ with 1NT if you hold:

   ♠ 9 3   ♡ 8 4   ◇ Q J 9 7 6 4 3   ♣ 5 2

vi) A psyche in a lower ranking suit when you have a good fit with partner can be effective. At green vulnerability partner opens 1♠ first in hand and your right-hand opponent doubles. Try 2♡ with:

   ♠ 10 9 7 5 4   ♡ 8 3   ◇ 9 5 3   ♣ 10 6 2

If you do pick an opportune moment to psyche you are unlikely to fool opponents as to their combined point count, but you may succeed in diverting them from their best strain. A judicious non-vulnerable 1♠ opening on the hand below has a sporting chance of getting vulnerable opponents to spend several rounds of bidding confirming that they hold spade guards, and finally settle in 3NT + 1 when 4♠ + 2 or 6♠ was available if they had discovered their 5-4 fit.

   ♠ 9 5   ♡ J 7 2   ◇ 10 9 6 5 4 2   ♣ 9 4

vii) Consider a *constructive* psyche! Suppose partner opens
1♠ and you have:

♠ K Q 8 5   ♡ 8   ◇ A K Q J 8 3   ♣ 5 2

A jump shift to 3♣ (Yes, I do mean three clubs!) before
Blackwooding your way into 6♠ may deflect a killing club lead.
Of course if Blackwood confirms that your side holds all the aces
you will bid the grand slam. In similar circumstances a false cue
bid can achieve the same result.

Finally one word of warning. Consider your purpose in playing
bridge! Psyching is a perfectly legal and ethical way of playing for
tops, but not everybody sees it that way. Many players resent
having their pockets picked by a psycher, and the regular psycher
is frequently less than popular in a predominately social club.
Also be wary of psyching if your partner is inexperienced. If he
behaves in an abnormal way that is deemed to have made
allowance for your psyche, the resulting adjusted score may be
very embarrassing to him. The fact that he is not good enough to
recognise what is, or isn't, normal will carry no weight with the
tournament director.

Playing for tops in card play

Once again there are plenty of opportunities for a slightly anti-
percentage line, indeed all the techniques you met earlier to
recover an individual board that was turning sour can also turn a
middle into a top (or bottom).

For example:

i) With ♠ 6 5 3 2 opposite ♠ A K J 4 play off the ♠ A K
rather than take a finesse.

ii) With ♠ 8 7 5 4 2 opposite ♠ A K J 3 take a second round
finesse of the ♠ J rather than play for the drop.

iii) With ♠ A K Q 10 opposite ♠ 8 6 3 finesse the ♠ 10 on the
third round.

iv) Play for a squeeze rather than a finesse for your contract.
Even if the odds are the same, the majority of the field will try the
finesse.

v) Try an abnormal opening lead.

vi) Consider whether a safety play might accomplish your
objective.